Psychology

TestPrep: DP Exam Practice Workbook

A note from us

While every effort has been made to provide accurate advice on the assessments for this subject, the only authoritative and definitive source of guidance and information is published in the official subject guide, teacher support materials, specimen papers and associated content published by the IB. Please refer to these documents in the first instance for advice and guidance on your assessments.

Any exam-style questions in this book have been written to help you practice and revise your knowledge and understanding of the content before your exam. Remember that the actual exam questions may not look like this.

SL & HL
Standard Level & Higher Level

Marcin Wielki

ReviseIB

Published by Extend Education Ltd., Alma House, 73 Rodney Road, Cheltenham, UK GL50 1HT

www.extendeducation.com

The right of Marcin Wielki to be identified as author of this work has been asserted by him with the Copyright, Designs and Patents Act 1988.

Reviewed by Reham Barghouti

Typesetting by York Publishing Solutions Pvt. Ltd., INDIA

Cover photo by Luis Felipe Lins on Unsplash

First published 2020

24 23 22 21 20

10 9 8 7 6 5 4 3 2 1

ISBN 978-1-913121-07-5

Other important information

A reminder that Extend Education is not in any way affiliated with the International Baccalaureate.

Many people have worked to create this book. We go through rigorous editorial processes, including separate answers checks and expert reviews of all content. However, we all make mistakes. So if you notice an error in the paper, please let us know at info@extendeducation.co.uk so we can make sure it is corrected at the earliest possible opportunity.

If you are an educator with a passion for creating content and would like to write for us, please contact info@extendeducation.co.uk or write to us through the contact form on our website www.extendeducation.co.uk.

CONTENTS

Permissions

Asch, S. E. (1951), "Effects of Group Pressure on the Modification and Distortion of Judgments", H. Guetzkow (Ed.), *Groups, Leadership and Men*, Pittsburgh, PA: Carnegie Press, pp. 177–190] p.15, Fagot, B, I., "The Influence of Sex of Child on Parental Reactions to Toddler Children", *Child Development*, Volume 49, Issue 2, pp. 459–465 p.52, Festinger, L, Riecken, H. W, Schachter, S. (1956), When Prophecy Fails: A Social and Psychological Study of a Modern Group that Predicted the Destruction of the World. Minneapolis: University of Minnesota Press, p.94, Feldman, R and Vengrober, A. (2011), "Posttraumatic Stress Disorder in Infants and Young Children Exposed to War-Related Trauma", *Journal of the American Academy of Child & Adolescent Psychiatry*, Volume 50, Issue 7, pp. 645–656 p.114

HOW TO USE THIS BOOK

This excellent exam practice book has been designed to help you prepare for your psychology exam. It is divided into three sections.

EXPLAIN

The EXPLAIN section gives you a rundown of your paper, including the number of marks available, how much time you'll have and the assessment objectives (AOs) and command terms. There's also a handy checklist of topics you can use as a revision checklist.

SHOW

The SHOW section gives you some examples of different questions you will come across in the exam. It's designed to help you learn the question types and the kinds of answers you can give to get you the maximum number of marks.

TEST

This is your chance to try out what you've learned. The TEST section has full sets of exam-style practice papers filled with the same type and number of questions that you can expect to see in the exam. The first set of papers has got a lot of helpful tips and suggestions for answering the questions. The middle set has more general advice – make sure you have revised before testing yourself with this set. The last set has no help at all. Not one single hint! Make sure you do this one a bit closer to your exam to check what else you might need to revise.

Set A

Paper 1 (SL/HL), Paper 2 (SL/HL) & Paper 3 (HL)

Presented with a lot of tips and guidance to help you get to the correct answer and boost your confidence!

Use these papers early on in your revision.

Set B

Paper 1 (SL/HL), Paper 2 (SL/HL) & Paper 3 (HL)

Presented with fewer helpful suggestions so you have to rely on your revision before trying these.

Test yourself using these papers when you're a bit more confident

Set C

Paper 1 (SL/HL), Paper 2 (SL/HL) & Paper 3 (HL)

Presented with space to add your own notes and no guidance – the perfect way to test you are exam ready.

Use these papers as close as you can to the exam.

All questions are presented with **ANSWERS** so you can check how you did in your practice papers.

Because answers are given for every question in Paper 2 – in Set A, Set B and C – you can actually test yourself on Paper 2 **12 times** for SL and **8 times** for HL!

Features

Take a look at some of the helpful features in these books that are designed to support you as you do your practice papers.

These will point you in the direction of the right answer!

These are general hints for answering the questions.

These are referred to as AOs all the way through this book

This box reminds you of the assessment objective being tested.

Beware of making common and easy-to-avoid mistakes!

These flag up common or easy-to-make mistakes that might cost you marks.

The command terms are like a clue to how you should answer your questions

COMMAND TERMS

These boxes outline what the command term is asking you to do.

For example, links to TOK or Extended Essay!

These show you when the questions have other interdisciplinary links.

These boxes contain really useful advice about what examiners are looking for

ANSWER ANALYSIS

These boxes include advice on how to get the most possible marks for your answer.

KNOWING YOUR PAPER

Knowing the requirements of your exam papers is as important as your knowledge about the topic. The structure of the paper shouldn't be a surprise to you during the exam session. Being familiarized with it will help you to answer the questions effectively.

How are you assessed?

You will sit two written papers for Standard Level and three written papers for Higher Level.

<table>
<tr><td></td><td>Standard Level</td><td>Higher Level</td></tr>
<tr><td rowspan="6">Paper 1</td><td>Section A: three short answered questions (SAQ)</td><td>Section A: three short answered questions (SAQ)</td></tr>
<tr><td>Section B: one extended-response question (ERQ)</td><td>Section B: one extended-response question (ERQ)</td></tr>
<tr><td>50% overall grade</td><td>40% overall grade</td></tr>
<tr><td>49 marks</td><td>49 marks</td></tr>
<tr><td>2 hours</td><td>2 hours</td></tr>
</table>

<table>
<tr><td></td><td>Standard Level</td><td>Higher Level</td></tr>
<tr><td rowspan="4">Paper 2</td><td>One extended-response question (ERQ)</td><td>Two extended-response questions (ERQ)</td></tr>
<tr><td>25% overall grade</td><td>20% overall grade</td></tr>
<tr><td>22 marks</td><td>44 marks</td></tr>
<tr><td>1 hour</td><td>2 hours</td></tr>
</table>

HL For Paper 3 you will answer three short answer questions on research methods taken from a list of six static questions. The stimulus material on qualitative or quantitative research method is provided.

<table>
<tr><td></td><td>Higher Level</td></tr>
<tr><td rowspan="4">Paper 3</td><td>Three short-answered questions (SAQ)</td></tr>
<tr><td>20% overall grade</td></tr>
<tr><td>24 marks</td></tr>
<tr><td>1 hour</td></tr>
</table>

HL ### Paper 3 – static questions

Question 1
You will always be asked the **same** questions:

1a. **Identify** the method used and **outline** two characteristics of the method. **[3 marks]**
1b. **Describe** the sampling method used in the study. **[3 marks]**
1c. **Suggest** an alternative or additional research method giving one reason for your choice. **[3 marks]**

Question 2
You will be asked **one** of the following two questions:
Describe the ethical considerations that were applied in the study and **explain** if further ethical considerations could be applied. **[6 marks]**
Describe the ethical considerations in reporting the results and **explain** ethical considerations that could be taken into account when applying the findings of the study. **[6 marks]**

Question 3
You will be asked **one** of the three questions:
Discuss the possibility of generalizing the findings of the study. **[9 marks]**
Discuss how a researcher could ensure that the results of the study are credible. **[9 marks]**
Discuss how the researcher in the study could avoid bias. **[9 marks]**

Paper 1, Section A requires you to answer three short answer questions on the core approaches to psychology. Each question is taken from one approach: biological, cognitive and sociocultural.

Paper 1, Section A is worth 27 marks.

SL For Section B you will need to answer one structured essay from three given options (one taken from each approach: biological, cognitive and sociocultural).

Paper 1, Section B is worth 22 marks.

HL In Paper 1, Section B the ERQs may reference the HL core extension.

In Paper 2, you will answer two essay questions. You must choose each one from a choice of three questions on two options: developmental psychology, abnormal psychology, psychology of human relationships, and health psychology.

SL In Paper 2, you will answer one essay question. You must choose one of three questions on one option: developmental psychology, abnormal psychology, psychology of human relationships, and health psychology.

Your assessment objectives

There are **three** assessment objectives for your IB psychology exam. Make sure you are clear on what you are expected to demonstrate for each one.

Assessment objective	Which questions test this?	Example questions
Assessment objective 1: KNOWLEDGE AND COMPREHENSION OF SPECIFIED CONTENT **COMMAND TERMS** AO1 questions will begin with describe and outline. Paper 3, Q1a will begin with the term identify.	Questions in the exam that test your understanding of AO1 are asking you to demonstrate knowledge and comprehension of different aspects of psychology: • key terms and psychological concepts • psychological theories and research studies • the biological, cognitive and sociocultural approaches to mental processes and behaviour • research methods used in psychology. Possible questions that might use AO1 command terms: Paper 1 Q1, Q2 and Q3 / Paper 3 Q1 and Q2	Paper 1, Q1: Outline how neural networks are formed, with reference to one study. **[9]** (HL only) Paper 3, Q1a: Identify the method used and outline two characteristics of the method. **[3]** Q1b: Describe the sampling method used in the study. **[3]** (HL only) Paper 3, Q2: Describe the ethical considerations that were applied in the study and explain if further ethical considerations could be applied. **[6]** **OR** Q3: Describe the ethical considerations in reporting the results and explain ethical considerations that could be taken into account when applying the findings of the study. **[6]**
Assessment objective 2: APPLICATION AND ANALYSIS **COMMAND TERMS** AO2 questions begin with explain. Paper 3, Q1c will begin with the term suggest.	Questions in the exam that test your understanding of AO2 are generally asking you to apply and analyse your knowledge, psychological theories (and/or studies). You may also be asked to use examples of psychological concepts to create an argument when answering a specific question.	Paper 1, Q3: Explain how **one** neurotransmitter influences **one** human behaviour. **[9]** (HL only) Paper 3, Q1c: Suggest an alternative or additional research method giving one reason for your choice. **[3]**

 COMMAND TERMS Q1–3 in Paper 1 will definitely include some AO1 questions (describe or outline) but you might get an AO2 question (for example, explain) in there.

 COMMAND TERMS Q2 in Paper 3 will be a **describe** question.

 COMMAND TERMS Q1 in Paper 3 will be split into three parts: • Q1a: Identify - AO1 • Q1b: Describe - AO1 • Q1c: Suggest - AO2

COMMAND TERMS Q1–3 will have a mixture of AO1 and AO2 questions. If you see 'Explain', then you know this is an AO2 question.

Assessment objective	Which questions test this?	Example questions
Assessment objective 3: SYNTHESIS AND EVALUATION **COMMAND TERMS** AO3 questions begin with contrast, discuss, evaluate or to what extent	Questions in the exam that test your understanding of AO3 are asking you to evaluate the contribution of psychological theories and/or research to understanding human behaviour. You might be asked to assess the value of the theories and/or studies in areas of applied psychology.	Paper 1, Q4–6: To what extent is **one** cognitive process reliable? **[22]** Paper 2, Q1–12: Discuss research on the theory. **[22]** (HL only) Paper 3, Q3: Discuss the possibility of generalizing/transferring the findings of the study.**[9]** **OR** Discuss how a researcher could ensure that the results of the study are credible.**[9]** **OR** Discuss how the researcher in the study could avoid bias. **[9]**

COMMAND TERMS
Q4–6 in Paper 1, the whole of Paper 2 and Q3 in Paper 3 will have AO3 command terms.

Before you begin your exam

Check that you have good knowledge and understanding of the topics before you undertake your exams. You could try Sets A and B during your revision to see which areas you need to work on, and Set C after your revision to check that you are ready for the exam.

Below is a checklist of core content for your DP psychology exam. Put a tick in the box when you have studied the topic, when you have learnt relevant case studies to reference in your exam, and when you are confident in your understanding and use of terminologies.

Topic	Studied	Research	Terminologies
Biological approach to behaviour			
The brain and behaviour	☐	☐	☐
Hormones and behaviour	☐	☐	☐
Genetics and behaviour	☐	☐	☐
(HL only) Animal research	☐	☐	☐
Cognitive approach to behaviour			
Cognitive processes	☐	☐	☐
Reliability of cognitive processes	☐	☐	☐
Emotion and cognition	☐	☐	☐
(HL only) Cognitive processing in digital world	☐	☐	☐

Topic	Studied	Research	Terminologies
Sociocultural approach to behaviour			
The individual and the group	☐	☐	☐
Cultural origins of behaviour and cognition	☐	☐	☐
Cultural influences on individual attitudes, identity and behaviours	☐	☐	☐
(HL only) The influence of globalization on individual attitudes, identities and behaviour	☐	☐	☐

What to do in your exam

Write your candidate session number on the exam paper.

Put your pen down and take a deep breath.

Scan through the exam from start to finish: make sure the last page of questions is the last page!

Carefully read the instructions for every part of the exam.

Read the question carefully. Identify the command term: what does the question require you to do?

Quickly outline your argument **before** you start writing.

Make sure to proofread your answers.

Use all the time you have. Don't rush!

COMMAND TERMS

Outline, **describe** and **explain** might be used in short-answer questions (SAQs).

For SAQs always provide **one** piece of research (empirical study).

COMMAND TERMS

Contrast, **discuss**, **evaluate** and **to what extent** will only be used in essay questions.

Aim to include **more than one** piece of research in your extended-response question (ERQ) to earn full marks. You should evaluate the research used in your response.

For the ERQ you should write an introduction and answer the question in your thesis statement. You should also include a definition of any terms used to respond to the question, and end with a clear and brief conclusion.

For SAQs and ERQs after each piece of evidence, you must link the study back to the question. Use the PEEL principle: point, evidence, explanation, link.

SHOWING WHAT YOU KNOW

We have included some model student answers in this section to give you an idea of how you should approach each question type in the exam. These are not the only possible answers, but should help you to identify a good approach when sitting your exam. There is also an explanation of why they are good examples, along with some tips, advice and common mistakes you should be mindful of when answering a question. You could try answering the exam-style questions yourself before looking at what the student has written. Then compare your answers with the ones given. Check to see if there are places where you could have communicated more effectively or used more appropriate language and terms.

Your Paper 1 questions

In Paper 1, you will need to answer three short questions (Section A) and one question with an extended-essay response (Section B). We have given you an example of a full-mark answer for each question below, so you can get familiar with the question types and how to best approach them.

Section A

Sociocultural approach to understanding behaviour

1. Explain social identity theory, making reference to one relevant study. **[9]**

Social identity theory is a hypothesis that analyses intergroup relationships in humans. The first step involves social categorization in which people are grouped together by shared characteristics. A group that one belongs to is an ingroup and a group that one doesn't belong to is an outgroup. The next step involves social comparison, which consists of groups comparing each other to maintain a positive social identity. Social identity is how someone sees themselves in relation to their memberships of a group. Ensuring a positive self-identity is a key point of intergroup relationships. One study that explored social identity theory is Tajfel (1970), which investigated if intergroup discrimination would take place based on group membership.

Tajfel (1970) is a laboratory experiment which had a sample of 64 schoolboys aged 14–15 from a Bristol school. The boys were told that the experimenters were interested in the study of visual judgements. Then they were shown different clusters of varying numbers of dots and asked to estimate how many dots they thought there were. The boys were then randomly assigned into groups and told it was based on whether they were an over-estimator or under-estimator in the previous task. Once in groups, they were asked to allocate small sums of money between the

EXPLAIN

This answer has included all features of social identity theory.

ANSWER ANALYSIS

This student has given an example of a study (Tajfel (1970)). They have also made sure to link the results of it back to the theory in the final sentence of their answer. This ensures the study is relevant to the question, which means they get the marks.

Do not confuse **social identity theory** with **social cognitive theory**.

AO2 applies to this type of question.

EXPLAIN

This requires you to give a detailed account, including reasons and causes of social identity theory.

ANSWER ANALYSIS

This answer would earn marks from the highest mark band [7–9]. Social identity theory is well explained in clear language and the study used is relevant and detailed. And it links back to the theory.

groups. The researchers found that the boys were more likely to give more money to their own groups, which shows a feature of social identity theory known as ingroup favouritism (the tendency to favour one's own group). The researchers then concluded that even if groups are arbitrary, humans still follow this categorization and tend to present outgroup discrimination. This is in line with social identity theory, and thus demonstrates how social identity theory can affect human behaviour.

Section B

Sociocultural approach to understanding behaviour

6. Discuss how one cultural dimension can influence one or more human behaviour. [22]

This essay will discuss the influence of cultural dimensions on human behaviour by examining research studies that have investigated this issue. Culture is a network of beliefs, traditions, rules and accepted norms followed by a group. Within cultures exist cultural dimensions, which are aspects of culture that can be compared relative to each other. A dimension represents the preference to one type of behaviour in a given culture. One cultural dimension is individualism vs collectivism, which is the extent to which a culture values individuals taking care of themselves and not demonstrating dependency on others (individualism) or seeing individuals as members of social groups that take care of each other in exchange for loyalty (collectivism). These different values are learned through a process of socialization (the internalization of cultural norms). The dimension 'I-C' and its influence on human behaviour was examined by Berry in 1967. The researcher examined how said dimension affects the behaviour of conformity in humans. Conformity is unspoken pressure on an individual to act or think like members of a group. Another cultural dimension is short-term orientation vs long-term orientation, which refers to the extent that a culture values short-term gratitude and results or long-term processes and traditions. Short-term-oriented societies focus on traditions, investments and sustained processes less than long-term-oriented societies. Another study which investigated I-C

Use only one dimension in your answer.

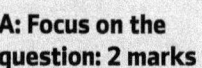

ANSWER ANALYSIS

A: Focus on the question: 2 marks

The answer is focused on the requirements of the question.

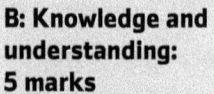

ANSWER ANALYSIS

B: Knowledge and understanding: 5 marks

The knowledge is detailed and psychological vocabulary is accurately used and relevant.

dimension is Petrova et.al (2007). Both studies have investigated the influence of cultural dimension on a human behaviour.

It is important to study cultural dimensions and how given behaviours vary depending on the culture so that these values can be respected by others on different occasions (for example, when interacting with other international companies). The incorporation of important beliefs in a cultural dimension can facilitate more successful communication and a better relationship. Psychologists have examined cultural dimensions through studies on different cultures in order to find their influence on behaviour.

Berry (1967) is a lab experiment with the aim of investigating how dimension I-C influenced the behaviour of conformity. The sample consisted of Tenme people of Sierra Leone (who are part of a collectivist culture) and Inuit people of Canada (who are part of an individualist society). It recreated the Asch's (1955) paradigm experiment. Each individual was brought into a room by him or herself and some confederates. For the test, they were given a set of nine lines. They were asked to match the line that most closely matched another line. Each of the participants stated their opinion aloud. The researchers found that the majority of Tenme people demonstrated conformity in their answer to match the rest of the group. Conversely, they found that only a small part of the Inuit people conformed their answer to the rest of the group. The researchers thus concluded that since the Tenme culture was a collectivist with agricultural economy and valued cooperation, the conformity behaviour will be a common phenomenon. They also concluded that since Inuit culture is individualistic and emphasizes self-sufficiency in practices such as child rearing, conformity is not a common behaviour. Thus this study illustrates the role of cultural dimension in human behaviour.

Petrova et al (2007) prepared the study to investigate if I-C dimension affects the level of compliance between cultures. She focused on the foot-in-the-door technique. For this study, a sample of 3,000 Asian and US students were asked to take part in a short voluntary online survey about relationships. One month after the survey, participants received a request to take part in another survey, which would take more time than the previous one

ANSWER ANALYSIS

C: Use of research to support answer: 5 marks

The research used is relevant. Both studies are well presented with a link to the requirements of the question.

ANSWER ANALYSIS

D: Critical thinking: 5 marks

The answer demonstrates well-developed critical thinking: evaluation and discussion of cultural dimension is consistent throughout.

ANSWER ANALYSIS

E: Clarity and organization: 2 marks

The answer is well organized with introduction, main body and conclusion.

ANSWER ANALYSIS

This student has used three studies to illustrate the role of cultural dimension. You should use **at least** two.

! The cultural dimension is named, but not described appropriately.

! More than one cultural dimension is described; this affects the organization of the answer and the focus.

(40 minutes instead of 20minutes). Compliance with the initial request had a stronger impact on subsequent compliance among the US participants than among the Asian participants. The findings of stronger consistency with past choices in individualistic cultures than in collectivistic cultures suggest that the stronger the cultural orientation toward individualism, the stronger the effect of past personal commitments on future compliance. That is, once participants have chosen to comply with a request, individualists should be more likely than collectivists to comply with subsequent, similar requests. This study shows that I-C cultural dimension affects human behaviour in terms of the level compliance.

When discussing cultural dimensions, one needs to remember that it's difficult to measure them effectively as these are subjective constructs. What is more, the theory of cultural dimensions could be applied to different aspects of your life. There also could be some difference within the culture as some individuals living in, for example, individualistic cultures, could show more collectivistic features since they originally were raised in the latter. When it comes to research, many studies are artificial in nature so it's not possible to generalize them to natural settings. There is the question in terms of how does the researcher's attitude and their own biases affect the whole procedure of the study and the results.

The concept of individualism/collectivism has a profound impact on a variety of domains of human behaviour. Both studies provide evidence for the impact of individualism/collectivism on the human tendency to act in accord with previous choices and its impact on conformity. By investigating these cross-cultural differences, the present findings advance our knowledge in cross-cultural research.

The studies are not explicitly linked to the dimension.

AO3 applies here.

DISCUSS

This requires you to offer a considered and balanced review, supported by appropriate research evidence, of how one cultural dimension influences one or more human behaviours.

ANSWER ANALYSIS

This answer would earn marks in the highest mark band (20 marks out of 22).

Your Paper 2 questions

Your Paper 2 will be made up of extended-response questions, which are worth 22 marks each.

1. Discuss one or more research methods used in the study of personal relationships. [22]

   Research dedicated to personal relationships create complications in terms of methodology, as it usually relies on reported abstract terms (such as level of love or satisfaction) given by participants which are impossible to measure directly.

DISCUSS

This requires you to offer a considered and balanced review (supported by appropriate research evidence) of one or more research methods in personal relationships.

One of the most common research methods in studies on personal relationships is the questionnaire. It consists of a list of questions which are asked to respondents. It is often used as a substitute for an interview, allows researchers to gather data from a large sample of people, and there is no need for the researchers to be present while participants fill them out.

In one of the studies, David Buss in 1989 aimed to rate the most desirable characteristics of a potential partner and hence to some extent explain the mechanism of determining which person is a good candidate for a relationship. The researcher gave a questionnaire containing three parts to a large number of participants (over 10,000) from 37 countries. The first part of the questionnaire asked for bibliographical data, such as country of origin, age, gender, etc. The second part asked to determine the perfect age difference between partners and desirable age of the partner. The last part asked participants to rate 18 characteristics in terms of their importance in a potential mating partner.

The results presented that women tend to choose older partners while men choose younger ones (results were compared with actual marriage statistics). Moreover, women rated prestige, industriousness and social status higher while men valued attractiveness and youth most. This led to the conclusion that females are looking for mature and experienced partners (hence the age difference) with a stable financial and social situation – perfect father material. Men are looking for attractive young women – who have high chances of giving birth to healthy offspring.

The use of a questionnaire allowed the researcher to gather a large amount of data in a shorter period of time than it would take if, for example, interviews were chosen as a research method. Three stages provided information necessary in determining results (e.g. age of participant vs desired age of a partner). Moreover, as the participants were asked to rate given characteristics, not list them by themselves, it was easier for researchers to conduct the analysis since they already had clearly stated numeric data, which they just had to compare. Additionally, the presence of researchers was not affecting the answers in a large extent as in the case of interviews, where the presence of other people asking about private topics could be intimidating for participants and could increase the risk of demand characteristics.

ANSWER ANALYSIS

A Focus on the question: **2 marks**

The answer is focused on the requirements of the question.

ANSWER ANALYSIS

B Knowledge and understanding: **6 marks**

The knowledge is detailed. Psychological vocabulary is accurately used and relevant.

ANSWER ANALYSIS

C Use of research to support answer: **5 marks**

The research used is relevant and both studies are well presented with a link to the requirements of the question.

ANSWER ANALYSIS

D Critical thinking: **5 marks**

The answer demonstrates well-developed critical thinking: evaluation and discussion of research methods is consistent throughout.

ANSWER ANALYSIS

E Clarity and organization: **2 marks**

The answer is well organized with introduction, main body and conclusion.

However, the use of the questionnaire has its limitations. Participants were from 37 countries, which meant that some of them were not native English speakers. They could have problems understanding given characteristics or emotionally associate them in a different way (e.g. chastity, which can be understood in more than one way, both positively and negatively, and as a result could have affected its importance in rating). Moreover, the questionnaire does not take cultural differences under consideration. Traits desired by American or British people may not be as important for Indian or Asian people. As there was no pressure coming from the presence of interviewer, the screw-you effect could possibly occur, meaning participants could fill the questionnaire with random information without real intent to participate in the study. There is also the possibility of each participant guessing the aim and giving the results which are (in their opinion) expected of them (demand characteristics).

The same research method is commonly used in studies focusing directly on marriages. In 2007, Markey & Markey conducted a study with the aim to identify the similarity and its significance in the choice of a partner. Using questionnaires, researchers asked about 200 people to describe psychological characteristics of their ideal partner. Then they were supposed to describe themselves. The results showed that participants' descriptions of an ideal partner were very similar to the description of themselves. In the second part of the study Markey et al. asked over 100 couples who had been together for at least a year to fill out the questionnaire about themselves and their partner's characteristics. Results were similar to the first part of the study; the findings were that participants prefer partners similar to themselves. So, the study shows that similarity plays a significant role in mate choice as we have a tendency to look for some similar characteristics which could help us to create a satisfying relationship.

The research method was a questionnaire. This way of gathering data is always based on self-reports, which are subjective in nature as it is very difficult to accurately describe yourself without being biased. Participants could think that they needed to put themselves in a good light as well as their partner because this was something that researchers expect. On the other hand, the use of this RM was a quick and convenient way to gather needed data, as for example using interviews instead would be more time consuming with the need

You should use **at least** one research method in this type of answer. Follow the instructions in the question.

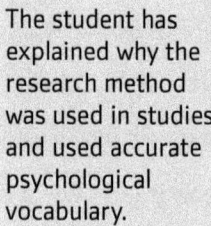

ANSWER ANALYSIS

The student has explained why the research method was used in studies and used accurate psychological vocabulary.

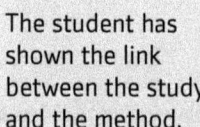

Make sure to use studies which demonstrate the research method of your choice.

ANSWER ANALYSIS

The student has shown the link between the study and the method.

AO3 is being tested in this question.

ANSWER ANALYSIS

This answer would earn marks in the highest mark band (20 out of 22 marks).

to transcribe information afterwards. It could be that people being asked about this kind of personal information would not disclose as much as they did by filling out questionnaires. People could rate their partners higher as they were intimidated by the question. However, the use of questionnaire allowed access to data in large numbers from many countries in a short period of time. They minimize the influence of researcher's presence on the answers given by participants and provide results which are easy to analyse. Questionnaires are also easily accessible by the participants and can be published online and advertised.

The research on personal relationships contains mainly abstract terms and definitions which are impossible to be measured directly. Questionnaires allow allocation of data in the research (e.g. by rating terms) which makes it possible to analyse. This research method also has its limits and there is a large possibility of bias occurring. Overall the questionnaire is a good method of research, but it should not be taken for a completely reliable source of information.

Your Paper 3 questions (HL only)

If you do HL, your final paper will be based on stimulus material.

Stimulus material

Solomon Asch (1951) conducted an experiment to study conformity. 50 men, students from Swarthmore College in the USA took part in the vision test. Participants had to assess the length of the line. Asch placed the participant in the room together
5 with seven other people – collaborators of the experimenter. Confederates previously agreed to provide specific answers during the task. The actual participant did not know that the other people cooperated with the researcher. Each person had to say which line (A, B or C) was most similar to the target line.
10 The answer was obvious every time. The real participant sat at the end and answered last. The experiment consisted of 18 trials, and confederates gave incorrect answers in 12 cases. Asch was interested in whether the real participant would agree with the majority's point of view. The results showed that 32% of
15 the real participants agreed with the unequivocally incorrect answer. During 12 attempts, about 75% of real participants gave the wrong answer at least once, and 25% didn't conform. In the control group, without the pressure to conform, in less than 1% of cases the participants gave the wrong answer.

[Source: Asch, S. E. (1951), "Effects of Group Pressure on the Modification and Distortion of Judgments", H. Guetzkow (Ed.), *Groups, Leadership and Men*, Pittsburgh, PA: Carnegie Press, pp. 177–190]

1. Describe the ethical considerations in conducting the study and explain additional ethical considerations that could be taken into account when conducting the study. **[6]**

Deception and psychological harm are two main ethical issues in this study. Asch deceived his participants by not telling them the real aim of the study and pretending that it was a vison test. This was to some extent justified as it let Asch get genuine answers without demand characteristics.

Another ethical issue was psychological harm. Real participants could have felt uncomfortable and stressed when giving answers against the group, which could lead them to change their opinion in the end. It could cause some long-term negative psychological consequences.

Two additional ethical considerations which could be taken into account are: right to withdrawal and anonymity.

The results of this study should be anonymous, especially when some sensitive aspects of the participant's functioning were taken under consideration (in this study, some participants could feel uncomfortable if their personal data was revealed). The identity of participants should not be known outside of the study.

Participants should always have the right to withdraw from a study at any time if they feel uncomfortable with any part of it. In this experiment, deception was used so no informed consent was given, and participants were not aware of their right to resign at any point of the study.

💬 **DESCRIBE**

This requires that you give a detailed account of the ethical considerations in the study.

💬 **EXPLAIN**

This requires detailed information about possible further ethical considerations used in the study.

ANSWER ANALYSIS

The student has divided their answer into two parts to ensure they get full marks. This makes it clear they have referred to:

1. Existing ethical considerations taken.
2. Considerations not mentioned in the study description.

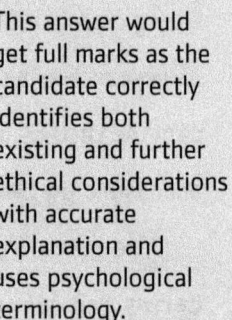

This is an example of one of the static questions that can be asked in Paper 3.

ANSWER ANALYSIS

This answer would get full marks as the candidate correctly identifies both existing and further ethical considerations with accurate explanation and uses psychological terminology.

For this type of question you need to demonstrate the knowledge about research methods in psychology.

Use the essay structure when answering questions.

ANSWER ANALYSIS

This question is worth 6 marks overall. There are 3 marks available for applied ethical considerations and 3 for additional considerations that were not necessarily used in the stimulus material.

AO1 applies to this type of question.

TESTING WHAT YOU KNOW

In this section, you will be able to test yourself with different sets of practice papers under exam conditions. By taking these mock papers, you will build your confidence and be able to identify any areas you need a bit more practice on. Set A (Paper 1 (SL and HL), Paper 2 (SL and HL) and Paper 3 (HL)) have a lot of additional guidance in the margin to help you get to the right answer, so attempt Set A first.

All you need is this book, a timer, a pen and some extra paper to use if you run out of answer lines. Then you can check your answers at the back of the book when you're done.

Take a deep breath, set your timer, and good luck!

Set A

Paper 1: Standard Level and Higher Level

- Set your timer for **2 hours**
- There are 49 marks available
- Answer ALL the questions

Section A

Answer all **three** questions in this section. Marks will be awarded for focused answers demonstrating accurate knowledge and understanding of research.

Biological approach to understanding behaviour

1. Describe the formation of neural networks with reference to **one** study. **[9]**

> You need to explain what neural networks are and how they are formed.

> The study used should be relevant and explained (aim, procedure, results and findings).

> The relevance of the study means that it should clearly illustrate how neural networks are formed.

> At the end of the study description should be an explicit link which will identify the creation of neural networks.

ANSWER ANALYSIS

The aim of the answer is to describe how neural networks are created by using one piece of research (one study).

AO2 applies here.

....

Do not only describe the study. It is most important to also refer to neural networks.

Two possible studies you could use are Maguire (2000) and Draganski (2004).

Cognitive approach to understanding behaviour

2. Explain the Multistore Memory Model with reference to **one** study. [9]

....

You need to explain the Multistore Memory Model (MSM).

The study used should be relevant and explained (aim, procedure, results and findings).

The relevance of the study means that it should clearly refer to MSM.

Two possible studies you could use are Glanzer and Cunitz (1966) or Milner (1966).

ANSWER ANALYSIS

The aim of the answer is to explain MSM by using one piece of research (one study). Explanation should be detailed and refer to the most important factors.

Do not only describe the study. You need to use it to illustrate MSM.

AO2 applies here.

....
....
....
....

Sociocultural approach to understanding behaviour

3. Explain how culture and cultural norms influence behaviour. [9]

....
....
....
....
....
....
....
....
....
....
....
....
....
....
....
....
....
....
....
....
....
....
....
....
....

EXPLAIN

This command term requires you to give a detailed account, including reasons and causes of the Multistore Memory model.

ANSWER ANALYSIS

The aim of the answer is to explain what culture and cultural norms are. Another important factor is to explain their influence on human behaviour.

Begin with a definition/ explanation of what is meant by the terms culture and cultural norms before describing a relevant study in support of your answer.

If you use other terms (such as acculturation or enculturation) remember to explain them.

Two possible relevant studies: Wang and Mallinckrodt (2006) and Ibañez (2015).

Don't just describe the study. You must also illustrate the role of culture and cultural norms and link it back to the study to get full marks.

AO2 applies here.

EXPLAIN

This command term requires you to give a detailed account of culture and cultural norms and how they influence behaviour.

If you choose to answer question 4 in this section, there is an SL version on this page and an HL version on the next page. Pick the one that is relevant to you.

SL Only choose this Q4 if you are an SL student. The HL option is shown after this one.

Section B

Answer **one** question in this section. Marks will be awarded for demonstration of knowledge and understanding (which requires the use of relevant psychological research), evidence of critical thinking (for example, application, analysis, synthesis, evaluation) and organization of answers.

4. **(SL option)** Discuss the role of pheromones on human behaviour. **[22]**

DISCUSS

The command term **discuss** requires you to give a balanced analysis (general discussion) with the use of a range of arguments. The discussion should look at general problems/issues of the phenomenon with reference to research and the theory (pheromones) itself.

Studies used should be relevant and explained (aim, procedure, results and findings).

Remember, pheromones are chemicals released to the environment by a member of one species and received by another individual of the same species. What other information about pheromones can you include here to give a detailed explanation?

Don't forget that the relevance of studies means that these should explicitly show the role of pheromones in human behaviour.

When giving arguments/ counterarguments remember to link them back to the theory (pheromones)

Two possible studies to be used are (but are not limited to): Wedekind et. al (1995), McClintock (1971), Hare (2017), Roberts et al. (2008).

ANSWER ANALYSIS

The response should be well structured to earn full marks for Criterion E.

ANSWER ANALYSIS

The aim of the answer is a balanced discussion of the role of pheromones in human behaviour with reference to empirical research.

Assessment objective 3 applies here.

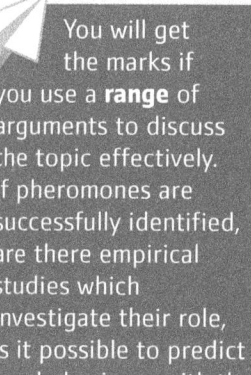

You will get the marks if you use a **range** of arguments to discuss the topic effectively. If pheromones are successfully identified, are there empirical studies which investigate their role, is it possible to predict any behaviours with the use of this theory?

4. **(HL option)** Discuss ethical considerations in animal research on the brain and behaviour. **[22]**

HL Only choose this Q4 if you are an HL student. The SL option is shown on the previous two pages.

DISCUSS

This command term requires you to offer a considered and balanced review, supported by appropriate research evidence of ethical considerations in animal research on the brain and behaviour.

Your introduction needs to focus on the question – remember to outline the argument.

Links to human behaviour should be explicitly identified throughout the answer.

Consider the role of organizations such as the British Psychological Society and the American Psychological Association.

You should include explicit information about how and why animal studies are used to help in understanding human behaviour.

Underline key words in the question to ensure you stay focused. Your evaluation of research studies should address ethical aspects to earn full marks.

Studies used in this answer should refer to areas such as: localization of function, neuroplasticity or neurotransmission.

Psychological terminology should be used accurately and properly explained. For example, neuroplasticity is the brain's ability to continuously change throughout someone's life.

You must include **two** relevant studies of animal research with reference to human behaviour. These should be described and related back to the question.

Some possible studies you could use are Merzenich et al (1984), Rosenzweig, Bennet, Diamond (1972), Martinez & Kesner (1991), and Rogers & Kesner (2003).

It is not enough to just describe animal studies. You must also discuss the relevant ethical considerations.

Don't include personal feelings in your answer. You must approach each topic with an impersonal balanced view.

AO3 applies here.

ANSWER ANALYSIS

Your answer should aim to analyse the reasons of animal research, possible alternatives and ethical problems (such as undue stress or harm).

5. To what extent is **one** cognitive process reliable? [22]

ANSWER ANALYSIS

The aim of the answer is to identify the extent to which one cognitive process is reliable. Both sides of the argument should be presented to show a balanced discussion and relevant knowledge.

You are being asked to write about **one** cognitive process (for example, memory).

Two studies have to be used for this answer. One needs to show that your chosen cognitive process is reliable and the other one must show that it is not reliable.

Remember to explain all the terms you use in your essay. For example, you might use the term 'flashbulb memory', which means a vivid memory associated with a significant event.

If you have chosen memory as your cognitive process you could use Loftus & Palmer (1974), Loftus, Miller, Burns (1978), Bartlett (1932) or Loftus & Pickerell (1995) to show that it is not reliable. Yuille & Cutshall (1986) is a good example for it being reliable.

Do not just discuss or evaluate research on one cognitive process. You need to examine how reliable it is and come to a conclusion in order to answer the question successfully.

Remember to include studies from both sides of the argument.

AO3 applies here.

TO WHAT EXTENT

This type of question requires a conclusion: how strong is the argument that one cognitive process is reliable, and what might other arguments be? Opinions and conclusions should be presented clearly and supported with appropriate evidence and a sound argument.

6. Evaluate research on social cognitive theory. [22]

Remember that you are evaluating the research on the theory and not the theory itself.

Possible studies to evaluate includes Bandura et al. (1961) on aggression in children and Joy, Kimball and Zabrack (1986) on the effect of TV on aggression in children.

That's it – your first Paper 1 practice is complete! Don't worry if you went over your timer. Reading the additional tips takes extra time. Make a note of any areas you found difficult and focus on those for your revision in the next few days. Make sure you take a bit of a break – don't go straight into Paper 2. It's important to recharge!

Paper 2: Standard Level and Higher Level

SL:
- Set your timer for **1 hour**
- There are 22 marks available
- Answer **one** question

HL:
- Set your timer for **2 hours**
- There are 44 marks available
- Answer **two** questions
  (from different options)

Abnormal psychology

1. Discuss the role of **one or more** clinical biases in diagnosis.　　　**[22]**

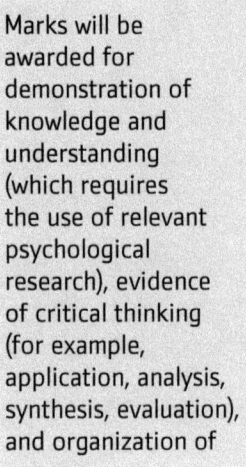

ANSWER ANALYSIS

Marks will be awarded for demonstration of knowledge and understanding (which requires the use of relevant psychological research), evidence of critical thinking (for example, application, analysis, synthesis, evaluation), and organization of answers.

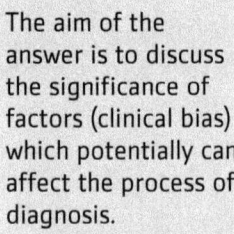

ANSWER ANALYSIS

The aim of the answer is to discuss the significance of factors (clinical bias) which potentially can affect the process of diagnosis.

You should know one or more of the following clinical biases: anchoring bias, confirmation bias, illusory correlation; cultural bias.

You could address the question by discussing what is meant by a clinical bias and providing examples of the role they play in diagnosis.

A link should be made between at least two clinical biases and diagnosis with reference to research studies and theories.

Relevant studies include Friedlander & Stockman (1983), Temerlin (1970), Mendel (2011), Swami (2012), Johnstone (1989), Li-Repac (1980), Burr (2002), Angel and Thoits (1987) and Yeung and Kam (2006).

Mendal (2011) studied 75 psychiatrists and 75 medical students to examine the effect of confirmation bias on mental health professionals.

Remember to examine the strengths and limitations of any studies discussed. For example, Li-Repac (1980) tested the role of stereotyping in diagnosis. She controlled age, socioeconomic status and level of pathology of the subjects, but was limited by a sample size of only 10.

Remember to explain all terms which will be used in your answer, such as clinical biases and diagnosis.

AO3 applies here.

DISCUSS

This requires you to offer a considered and balanced review of the role of one or more clinical biases in diagnosis.

2. Discuss a biological approach to explaining the aetiology of **one** disorder. [22]

You can use one explanation in detail from the biological approach with more than one study to show depth of knowledge **or** you can use several brief explanations from the biological approach to show breadth of knowledge.

Possible relevant studies include Kendler and Caspi.

3. Discuss **one** psychological treatment of **one** disorder. [22]

DISCUSS

This requires you to offer considered and balanced reviews of one psychological treatment (such as CBT) in the treatment of one psychological disorder (such as depression).

Discuss how the treatment works and the strengths and limitations of the treatment. Your response should **not** only focus on effectiveness.

Relevant research on anorexia includes Pike et al. (2003), Fairburn et al. (2015), Robin et al. (1999), Paulson-Karlsson et al. (2009) and Foerde et al. (2015).

Relevant research on depression includes Cuijpers et al. (2011), Elkin et al. (1989), Riggs et al. (2007) and Segal et al. (2010).

Relevant research for PTSD includes Weine (1998), Knaevelsrud et al. (2014), Alghamdi et al. (2014), Difede and Hoffman (2002), Rizzo et al. (2012) and Botella et al. (2015).

Developmental psychology

4. Evaluate **one** theory of cognitive development. [22]

....

....

....

....

....

....

....

....

....

....

....

....

....

....

....

....

....

....

....

....

....

....

....

....

....

....

....

....

....

....

....

....

....

ANSWER ANALYSIS

The aim of the answer is to present strengths and limitations of one theory of cognitive development.

You need to choose one theory of cognitive development (for example, Piaget's Theory or Vygotsky's Theory).

At least two studies should be used to illustrate your answer.

Your main focus should be on strengths and limitations of the theory.

You may address other theories and be awarded marks for these as long as they are clearly used to evaluate the main theory addressed in the answer.

Remember to explain all terms which will be used in your answer.

! The main focus of your answer should be on critical analysis of the theory – evaluation of studies should not be the main part of your answer.

! If you use focus on gender identity instead of cognitive development you won't be given credit as this is not what the question is asking you to do.

If you evaluate more than one theory, you will be given credit only for the first evaluation.

AO3 applies here.

EVALUATE

This requires you to make an appraisal by weighing up the strengths and limitations of one theory of cognitive development. Although a discussion of both strengths and limitations is required, it does not have to be evenly balanced to gain high marks.

When evaluating theories it is important to also look at practical applications and implications of the theory.

5. Discuss potential effects of deprivation and/or trauma on later development.

[22]

Possible relevant research includes Koluchova (1972), Chugani et al. (2001), Carion et al. (2009), Rutter et al. (2007), Curtiss (1974), Kreppner, O'Connor, Dunn & Andersen Wood (1999) and Bosquet-Enlow et al. (2012).

Physiology

6. Discuss research on attachment. [22]

Your main focus should be on analysis and discussion of research studies into attachment. You could start by defining what attachment is in psychological terms and explaining the relevance of it.

At least **two** studies should be used to illustrate your answer. However, it will not be useful to just list lots of studies without explaining their relevance.

An example of attachment is how babies strongly attach to their mothers. Another example is that of adult romantic attachment. The patterns of adult romantic attachment are the result of previous experiences during our childhood.

Remember to explain all terms which will be used in your answer. For example, if you talk about emotional processing you should start by defining that it is the ability to process stress and other extreme emotions in order to move past them.

The main focus of your answer should be on critical analysis of studies on attachment including their significance, application and strengths/limitations.

Every time when the question asks to evaluate research this means that you have to evaluate only studies, **not** theories.

Don't talk too much about attachment in biological terms. Your answer should talk about research and terms in psychology.

AO3 applies here.

DISCUSS

This requires you to offer a considered and balanced review of research studies into attachment. You should present your conclusions clearly and support them by appropriate evidence.

Possible relevant research includes Harlow (1958), Ainsworth (1970), Van Ijzendoorn and Kroonenberg (1988), Hazan and Shaver (1987), Simpson et al. (1996) and Fonagy et al. (1991).

Possible concepts to use for evaluation of research include operationalization of attachment, predictive validity, cross-cultural validity, use of prospective and retrospective research, and use of animal models.

Health psychology

7. Discuss the role of health beliefs as determinants of health. [22]

ANSWER ANALYSIS

The question is asking you to explain health beliefs and use studies to illustrate their role as determinants of health. It is not enough to only discuss health beliefs.

You could underline the words 'determinants of health' to help keep you focused on the question.

At least **two studies** should be used to illustrate your answer. One example you could use is Weinberger (1981), which studied opinions on smokers.

Optimism bias and self-efficacy are two health beliefs you could use. Optimism bias is a person's belief that they are more likely to experience a positive event than a negative one.

Remember to explain all the terms you use in your answer. For example, the cognitive approach assumes that our behaviour is influenced by our thought processes, memory, attention, decision making, perception, etc.

If you focus on evaluating the studies into health beliefs instead of discussing their significance then you will get low marks for your answer.

AO3 applies here.

DISCUSS

This requires you to offer a considered and balanced review of health beliefs with critical reference to their role as determinants of health.

8. Evaluate **one or more** studies related to explanations of **one or more** health problems. [22]

Remember to explain all the terms you use in your answer. For example, if you use stress and reference the Hans Selye General Adaptation Syndrome, you should include the three stages (alarm reaction, resistance and exhaustion).

If you focus on evaluation of theories instead of studies you will not be given credit for your answer.

AO3 applies here.

EVALUATE

This requires you to make an appraisal of one or more studies related to explanations of one or more health problems by weighing up the strengths and limitations. Although both strengths and limitations should be addressed, this does not have to be evenly balanced.

9. Discuss the effectiveness of **one or more** health promotion programmes. [22]

_____
_____
_____
_____
_____
_____
_____
_____
_____
_____
_____
_____
_____
_____
_____
_____
_____
_____
_____
_____
_____
_____
_____
_____
_____
_____
_____
_____
_____
_____

ANSWER ANALYSIS

Your answer should present critical analysis and evaluation of the effects of one or more health promotion strategies.

You could underline the word 'effectiveness' to help you focus as you write your answer.

You could start your answer by defining what 'health promotion' is. This might make it easier for you to discuss how effective the programmes were at encouraging it.

Health promotion programmes could be aimed at the person responsible for their own health, or at people responsible for other people's health (such as parents).

At least **two** studies should be included in your answer. You could use Black (2010), which investigated changes in bodies and habits during a 12-session health promotion.

As indicated in the question, you can focus on **one or more** health promotion strategy. One possible example is the Canadian THINK AGAIN campaign, which was aimed at parents of young children.

Remember to explain all terms which will be used in your answer. For example, health promotion is the process of enabling people to increase control over and improve their health.

Don't waste time evaluating studies. You need to explain and discuss how **effective** your chosen health promotion strategies are. However, if the evaluation of studies serves as an argument in discussion of effectiveness of health promotion strategies then it is fine. Just make sure to not spend too much time on this as criticism of research shouldn't be the main focus.

A03 applies here.

DISCUSS

This requires you to offer a considered and balanced review of effectiveness of one or more health promotion strategies. You should present your conclusions clearly and support them by appropriate evidence.

Psychology of human relationships

10. To what extent does the biological approach contribute to the understanding of personal relationships? **[22]**

TO WHAT EXTENT

It is appropriate and useful that you address sociocultural and/or cognitive factors in order to address this command term.

Biological factors in human relationships include evolutionary, genetic and neurochemical explanations.

You may consider a small number of biological factors in order to demonstrate depth of knowledge or may consider a larger number of biological factors in order to demonstrate breadth of knowledge. Both approaches are equally acceptable.

Studies which can be used are Buss (1989), Wedekind (1995) and Festinger et al (1950).

ANSWER ANALYSIS

Your answer should consider the contribution of biological factors to the understanding of personal relationships. You should also discuss counter arguments to be given full credit for your answer.

AO3 applies here.

TO WHAT EXTENT

This requires you to explain more than one approach to a given issue. Examiners expect you to determine which side of argument is more relevant and why.

Possible research includes Fisher et al. (2005), Walum et al. (2008), Ditzen et al. (2009), Low (1990) and Wedekind (1995).

11. Evaluate research into conflict/conflict resolution. **[22]**

Evaluation may include, but is not limited to:
- methodological, cultural, and gender considerations
- contrary and supporting findings
- applications of the research study
- ethical concerns regarding the study
- validity and reliability of the study.

Remember to explain all the terms which you use in your answer.

Two possible pieces of research you could use are Sherif (1954) and Howarth (2002).

AO3 applies here.

EVALUATE

This requires you to make an appraisal by weighing up the strengths and limitations of research into conflict/conflict resolution. Although a discussion of both strengths and limitations is required, it does not have to be evenly balanced to gain high marks.

Possible concepts to define include resource stress, Realistic Conflict Theory, Social Identity Theory, group polarization, contact hypothesis and Social Cognitive Theory.

Possible research to use includes Diab (1963), Sherif (1954), Esses et al. (2001), Stott et al. (2001), Novotny and Polansky (2011) and Paluck (2005).

12. Discuss prosocial behaviour. [22]

ANSWER ANALYSIS

This answer should focus on balanced analysis of a prosocial behaviour.

Arguments which can be used are: kin selection theory, negative state relief model, social exchange theory or empathy altruism model.

You might discuss the Elaine study – Batson (1981).

Remember to explain all the terms you use in your answer. For example, you might discuss altruism, which involves selflessly helping others.

Although you should have some evaluation of studies in your answer, this shouldn't be your main focus when answering this question.

AO3 applies here.

DISCUSS

This requires you to present a considered and balanced review of prosocial behaviour. You should present your conclusions clearly and support them by appropriate evidence.

Possible concepts to discuss include the social exchange theory, altruism, inclusive fitness, kin selection and the empathy-altruism model.

Possible research to use that overlap with Paper 1 Sociocultural Approach are Whiting & Whiting on the role of collectivistic culture, and Levine (2005) on in-group bias.

Paper 3: Higher Level

- Set your timer for **1 hour**
- There are 24 marks available
- Answer **all** the questions

The stimulus material below is based on a study on identity development.

Fagot (1978) performed a study to check if parents treat children differently when it comes to the child's gender. 24 families with one child between 20–24 months old took part. In the study, 12 of them had a son and 12 of them had one daughter.
5 Researchers observed children with their parents in their homes for five weeks. A checklist was used for 46 child behaviours and 19 parental reactions. Parents were told that the study was focused on child behaviour in general, there was no mention of gender significance. The parents gave more approval to the child when
10 the child was engaged in a same sex preferred behaviour and were more likely to give negative response to cross-gender behaviour. Parents reacted negatively when girls where engaged in 'too active' behaviours – motor activities (e.g. manipulating an object). More positive responses were given when girls were involved in
15 dependant behaviours, what is more girls asking for help was also considered positive, contradictory to boys. Researchers claim that parents didn't realize that they were using gender stereotypes.

[Source: Fagot, B, I., "The Influence of Sex of Child on Parental Reactions to Toddler Children", *Child Development*, Volume 49, Issue 2, pp. 459–465]

Answer **all** of the following three questions, referring to the stimulus material in your answer. Marks will be awarded for demonstration of knowledge and understanding of research methodology.

1a. Identify the method used and outline **two** characteristics of the method. **[3]**

....

....

....

....

....

....

....

....

....

....

....

....

Make sure to carefully read the stimulus material. Highlight or underline the most important parts if necessary.

Your answers should directly refer to the text. There is no need to quote: what you can do is count the lines of the text and refer to a specific line when answering the question.

Carefully read the questions. What command term is there? What are you expected to write about?

Make sure you know the meaning of every term used in the question.

ANSWER ANALYSIS

This answer should focus on the research method used in the stimulus material.

Remember not to give more than two characteristics of the method as you will not be given additional credit for it.

The characteristics of the method you identified could help you in differentiation between the one used in the study and other similar methods.

You should be very clear when identifying research methods as general terms will not be sufficient. For example, if a study used a 'semi-structured interview' then writing down 'interview' would not be specific enough.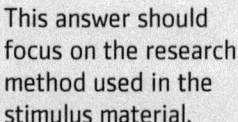

AO1 applies here.

1b. Describe the sampling method used in the study. [3]

1c. Suggest an alternative or additional research method giving **one** reason for your choice. [3]

2. Describe the ethical considerations that were applied in the study and explain if further ethical considerations could be applied. **[6]**

ANSWER ANALYSIS

You should focus on both aspects of ethical considerations to be awarded full marks.

ANSWER ANALYSIS

You could focus on informed consent, protection from harm, anonymity/ confidentiality, right to withdraw, deception and debriefing.

Remember to divide your answer into two paragraphs:
• Paragraph one: ethical considerations applied in the study
• Paragraph two: additional considerations.

Do not overdo one aspect of your answer (applied or additional ethical considerations).

AO1 and AO2 apply here.

DESCRIBE

This question requires you to give a detailed account of existing ethical issues and provide reasons for additional ethical considerations.

3. Discuss the possibility of generalizing/transferring the findings of the study. **[9]**

ANSWER ANALYSIS

You should focus on possible problems/ considerations in the attempt to generalize findings to wider population/ different settings.

Remember to refer to specific types of generalization when discussing possible arguments.

When answering these types of questions, remember to refer to stimulus material as this will make your answer more valid.

Be careful not to describe general issues with the study. Instead focus on generalization specifically.

AO3 applies here.

DISCUSS

This requires you to present a balanced review of possible generalization/ transferability of the findings from the given study.

Set B

Are you ready to tackle Set B? There are fewer helpful tips and suggestions for this set so make sure you have done some revision before you try out these papers.

Take at least a day's break between papers. Don't burn yourself out.

Have you remembered extra paper in case you run out of space?

Paper 1: Standard Level and Higher Level

- Set your timer for **2 hours**
- There are 49 marks available
- Answer ALL the questions

> **!** For Paper 1, Section B in this book, there are some question options that are just for SL students and some options just for HL students. These are clearly indicated so, if you choose to answer one of these, just make sure you pick the right one for your level.

Section A

Answer all **three** questions in this section. Marks will be awarded for focused answers demonstrating accurate knowledge and understanding of research.

Biological approach to understanding behaviour

1. Describe **one** study of the role of pheromones in human behaviour. **[9]**

> 💬 **DESCRIBE**
> This answer should contain a detailed description of the study and how it was conducted with reference to pheromones.

> The study used should be relevant and described (aim, procedure, results and findings).

> You should define what pheromones are in your answer.

> The relevance of the study means that it should clearly show the potential role of pheromones in human behaviour.

> At the end of study there should be an explicit link, which will identify the role of pheromones in human behaviour.

> Some possible studies you could use are Wedekind et. al (1995), Zhou et al. (2014) or Hare (2017).

ANSWER ANALYSIS

The aim of the answer is to demonstrate the role of pheromones in human behaviour by detailed explanation of one empirical research.

If you describe a study that is not directly linked to pheromones you will get low marks.

AO2 applies here.

Cognitive approach to understanding behaviour

2. Explain **one** cognitive bias in thinking and decision making. [9]

You should explain what is meant by a bias, and how this bias can lead to unreliability in a cognitive process. Why and how it happens should be outlined.

You need to use a study (including the aim, procedure and findings) to illustrate your explanation. However, there is no requirement for you to evaluate the study.

Possible research you could use:
- Englisch & Mussweiler (2001): anchoring bias
- Tversky & Kahnemann (1974): anchoring bias
- Tversky & Kahnemann (1974): availability heuristic
- Strack & Mussweiler (1997): anchoring bias
- Tversky & Kahneman (1986): framing effect
- Hill et al. (2008): confirmation bias
- Hamilton & Rose (1980): illusory correlation
- Risen et al. (2007): illusory correlation

Remember to make an explicit link between the study and the cognitive bias.

If you do not use a study, you will receive low marks as cognitive bias needs to be illustrated with empirical research.

Cognitive biases which you could use are: illusory correlation, confirmation bias, anchoring bias, framing effect, availability heuristic or representative heuristic.

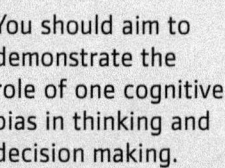

ANSWER ANALYSIS

You should aim to demonstrate the role of one cognitive bias in thinking and decision making.

AO2 applies here.

EXPLAIN

This question requires you to give a detailed account of one cognitive bias in thinking and decision-making.

If you write about two biases, you will only receive credit for the first explanation.

Sociocultural approach to understanding behaviour

3. Explain **one** ethical consideration relevant to one study of the individual and the group. [9]

💬 **EXPLAIN**

This requires you to give a detailed account of one ethical consideration of one empirical research.

📄 You need to use a study (including the aim, procedure and findings) to illustrate your explanation.

📄 You need to explain the ethical issue you will be referring to.

📄 You could use Bandura, Ross & Ross (1961) as a study in your answer.

ANSWER ANALYSIS

You should aim to demonstrate one ethical consideration in the study of the individual and the group.

❗ Do not forget to write about the study investigating the individual and the group.

🎯 AO2 applies here.

Section B

Answer **one** question in this section. Marks will be awarded for demonstration of knowledge and understanding (which requires the use of relevant psychological research), evidence of critical thinking (for example, application, analysis, synthesis, evaluation), and organization of answers.

4. Discuss **one** evolutionary explanation of **one** behaviour. [22]

You need to use at least **two** studies to illustrate your explanation.

Remember to make an explicit link between studies and one evolutionary explanation of behaviour.

You should also aim to write about the application of one explanation of behaviour.

Two possible studies are Fessler (2005) and Curtis, Aunger, Rabie (2004).

ANSWER ANALYSIS

You should aim to present an argument using evidence. Do not just evaluate research.

Remember to write about one evolutionary explanation.

If you decide to include animal research in your answer, you should make sure to identify the link between this research and human behaviour.

AO3 applies here.

EXPLAIN

You should offer a considered and balanced review of one evolutionary explanation of one behaviour. Conclusions should be presented clearly and supported by appropriate evidence.

5. (SL option) Discuss schema theory with reference to research studies. **[22]**

SL Only choose this Q5 if you are an SL student. The HL option is shown **after** this one.

Remember to explain schema theory and its assumptions.

Link this explanation to specific studies that investigate schema theory.

Potential studies to be used: Bartlett (1932), Loftus and Palmer (1974), Cohen (1990), Cohen & Oakes (1993), Bransford & Johnson (1972), Anderson & Pichert (1978), Brewer & Treyens (1981);

ANSWER ANALYSIS

The response should be well structured to earn full marks for Criterion E.

ANSWER ANALYSIS

The aim of the answer is to investigate different studies and general problems/arguments which refer to schema theory – usefulness of the theory (for example, is the theory descriptive or explanatory or does it have high predictive validity) and studies which are used in the response.

Assessment objective 3 applies here.

5. **(HL option)** Discuss how the use of digital technology affects **one** cognitive process. [22]

Only choose this Q5 if you are an HL student. The SL option is shown on the previous two pages.

Digital technology which you can use in your answer could be computers, phones, social media, video games and search engines.

You need to present relevant knowledge about the cognitive processes in general as well as the effect digital technology has on it.

At least **two studies** should be included in your answers (and described in detail) to illustrate the argument.

DISCUSS

Analyse and evaluate your evidence.

Link the argument back to the question as often as possible.

ANSWER ANALYSIS

You should aim to explain what the influence of digital technology is on one cognitive process.

If you focus on more than one cognitive process you will not be given credit for it, as this is not what you are asked to do. The examiner will only give you credit for the first cognitive process.

A03 applies here.

6. **(SL option)** Evaluate research on the role of cultural dimensions in behaviour.

SL Only choose this Q6 if you are an SL student. The HL option is shown **after** this one.

Cultural dimensions could include: power distance; individualism vs collectivism; masculinity vs femininity; uncertainty vs avoidance; long-term vs short-term orientation (Confucian work dynamism); monochronous vs polychronous time orientation.

You need to identify a link between the cultural dimension(s) and human behaviour, demonstrating what kind of effect the cultural dimension has on a given human behaviour.

You can focus on one or more cultural dimensions.

You need to explain cultural dimension(s) used in your response.

Potential arguments in evaluation of studies could include: critical approach to empirical studies investigating specific CD as well as application of the findings; potential biases in research and the theory; difficulties in the measurement and operationalization of cultural dimensions; methodological, cultural & ethical considerations of research.

Remember to include both strengths and limitations of research. However, these don't have to be evenly balanced.

Empirical studies to be used in this response: Berry (1967), Basset (2004), Hofstede (1984), Petrova (2007).

ANSWER ANALYSIS

The response should be well structured to earn full marks for Criterion E.

ANSWER ANALYSIS

The aim of the answer is to investigate different studies and general problems/arguments which refer to studies which examine cultural dimensions.

Assessment objective 3 applies here.

 COMMAND TERMS

The command term **evaluate** requires you to present strengths and limitations of research on the role of cultural dimensions in behaviour.

6. **(HL option)** Discuss how globalization may influence behaviour. **[22]**

HL / Only choose this Q6 if you are an HL student. The SL option is shown on the previous two pages.

To make sure that your answer is focused and meets the demands of the command term, remember to write topic sentences. Your answer should be illustrated by at least two relevant studies.

DISCUSS

You should offer a considered and balanced review that includes a range of arguments, factors or hypotheses regarding the effect of globalization on behaviour.

You may approach the question by explaining globalization and discussing positive and negative effects of it.

Studies you could use here are Gonzales et al (2004), Chen et al (2008) and Lyons-Padilla et al (2015).

ANSWER ANALYSIS

You should aim for a balanced discussion of influences of globalization on behaviour.

Remember to explain all relevant terms.

You should explicitly identify the link between the effect of globalization of specific behaviour and the empirical study (or theory).

AO3 applies here.

Paper 2: Standard Level and Higher Level

SL:
- Set your timer for **1 hour**
- There are 22 marks available
- Answer **one** question

HL:
- Set your timer for **2 hours**
- There are 44 marks available
- Answer **two** questions
  (from different options)

Marks will be awarded for demonstration of knowledge and understanding (which requires the use of relevant psychological research), evidence of critical thinking (for example, application, analysis, synthesis, evaluation) and organization of answers.

Abnormal psychology

1. Discuss concepts of normality and abnormality. [22]

Two empirical studies (research) you could use in this answer are Rosenhan (1973) and Li-Repac (1980).

Concepts of normality/abnormality which you can use in this answer may include but are not limited to: abnormality as a deviation from social norms; abnormality as statistical infrequency; six characteristics of mental health by Jahoda (1958); and seven criteria of abnormality by Rosenhan & Seligman (1984).

Answers may include, but are not limited to:
- cross-cultural issues
- gender biases
- research findings
- the issue of labelling
- historical perspectives on changing norms on normality (for example, changing views on homosexuality or political dissent)
- difficulties in defining normality/abnormality.

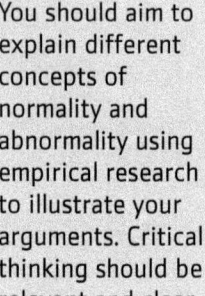

ANSWER ANALYSIS

You should aim to explain different concepts of normality and abnormality using empirical research to illustrate your arguments. Critical thinking should be relevant and clear.

ANSWER ANALYSIS

You may discuss a smaller number of concepts of normality and abnormality in order to demonstrate depth of knowledge, or discuss a larger number of concepts of normality and abnormality in order to demonstrate breadth of knowledge. Both approaches are equally acceptable.

! Do not introduce a new term without explaining it.

! Remember not to use theories or definitions as research: you will be expected to use studies.

! Aim to include two pieces of research to illustrate concepts of normality and abnormality.

AO3 applies here.

DISCUSS

You should offer a considered and balanced review that includes various concepts of normality and abnormality. Conclusions should be presented clearly and supported by appropriate evidence.

Abnormal psychology

2. Discuss prevalence rates and disorders. [22]

You could focus only on **one** disorder (e.g. depression or anorexia nervosa) or you could focus on **disorders in general**. Either method would be suitable.

You should explain any term you use in this answer.

At least two studies should be used in your answer.

ANSWER ANALYSIS

You should aim for a balanced discussion of prevalence rates of disorders.

ANSWER ANALYSIS

You should explicitly identify the link between studies used in your answer and prevalence rates of disorders.

Some of the studies can also be used in questions which refer to etiologies of disorders, so you need to make sure that you use them in an accurate context in this answer.

AO3 applies here.

DISCUSS

You should offer a considered and balanced review that includes a range of arguments, factors or hypotheses regarding the prevalence rates of disorders.

Abnormal psychology

3. Discuss **one or more** research methods in the study of the treatment of disorders. [22]

_____

(blank answer lines)

In some past papers from the IB, research methods might be referred to as 'approaches to research'.

Your focus should be on **one or more** research methods (interviews, case studies, observations or experiments) within the topic of treatment of disorders.

At least **two** studies should be used in your answer.

You should analyse strengths and limitations of one or two research methods of your choice.

ANSWER ANALYSIS

You should aim to analyse strengths and limitations of empirical research used in the treatment of disorders. Critical thinking should be relevant and clear.

Remember not to use theories or definitions as research. You should use studies.

AO3 applies here.

DISCUSS

Offer a considered and balanced review that includes different arguments in discussion of research method(s). Conclusions should be presented clearly and supported by appropriate evidence.

Developmental psychology

4. Discuss brain development in developing as a learner. [22]

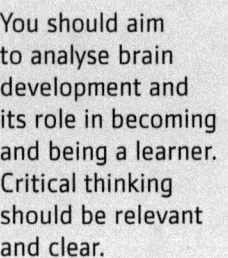

Your focus should be on the brain (such as neuroplasticity, localization of function or neurotransmission) and its significance as a base for cognitive development (in this case, developing as a learner).

At least **two** studies should be used in your answer.

ANSWER ANALYSIS

You should aim to analyse brain development and its role in becoming and being a learner. Critical thinking should be relevant and clear.

AO3 applies here.

DISCUSS

Offer a considered and balanced review that includes different arguments in discussion of the role of brain development in developing as a learner. Conclusions should be presented clearly and supported by appropriate evidence.

Developmental psychology

5. Discuss the potential role of poverty/socioeconomic status on development.

[22]

Your focus should be on poverty/ socioeconomic status and its effect on development.

At least **two** studies should be used in your answer.

ANSWER ANALYSIS

You should aim to analyse the significance of environmental influences (poverty/ socioeconomic status) in the context of development. Critical thinking should be relevant and clear.

A03 applies here.

DISCUSS

Offer a considered and balanced review that includes different arguments in discussion of the role of poverty/ socioeconomic status in development. Conclusions should be presented clearly and supported by appropriate evidence.

Developmental psychology

Developmental psychology

6. Discuss **one or more** gender identity theory.   [22]

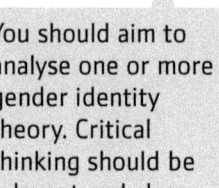

Your focus should be on balanced analysis of **one or more** gender identity theory.

At least **two** studies should be used in your answer.

Discuss a theory with the use of empirical studies for discussion and illustration.

ANSWER ANALYSIS

You should aim to analyse one or more gender identity theory. Critical thinking should be relevant and clear.

AO3 applies here.

DISCUSS

Offer a considered and balanced review that includes different arguments in discussion of one or more theory of gender identity. Conclusions should be presented clearly and supported by appropriate evidence.

Health psychology

7. Evaluate research on the role of risk and/or protective factors as determinants of health. **[22]**

Explain all terms which will be used in your answer.

At least two empirical studies should be used in your answer.

The topics related to health which you can use are:
- stress
- obesity
- addiction
- chronic pain
- sexual health.

ANSWER ANALYSIS

Your focus should be on evaluation of research studies on risk and/or protective factors and their role in health. For example, Cohen (1991) investigated how infections were affected by psychological stress.

You can focus only on risk/protective factors; however, if you decide to analyse both this will also be acceptable.

AO3 applies here.

EVALUATE

This requires you to discuss strengths and limitations of research on the risk and/or protective factors. Conclusions should be presented clearly and supported by appropriate evidence.

Health psychology

8. Evaluate **one or more** biological explanations of one health problem. [22]

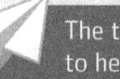
Explain all the terms which you use in your answer.

At least **two** empirical studies should be used in your answer. Make a quick note of the ones you will use when planning your answer.

The topics related to health are:
• stress
• obesity
• addiction
• chronic pain
• sexual health.

ANSWER ANALYSIS

Your focus should be on the evaluation of one or more biological explanation(s) of one health problem.

You won't get high marks if you only evaluate the studies used to illustrate your argument.

AO3 applies here.

EVALUATE

This requires you to discuss strengths and limitations of research on the risk and/or protective factors. Conclusions should be presented clearly and supported by appropriate evidence.

Health psychology

9. Discuss ethical considerations in the study of health promotion. **[22]**

Explain all terms which will be used in your answer.

At least two empirical studies should be used in your answer.

Studies used in this answer could be Akyuz (2014) and Horne et al (2004).

Relevant ethical considerations may include, but are not limited to:
- informed consent
- psychological harm
- anonymity
- right to withdraw
- deception
- debriefing.

ANSWER ANALYSIS

Your main focus should be on ethical considerations of research studies into health promotion.

This is asking you about the **study** of health promotion. Do not talk about the ethical considerations of health promotion in general.

AO3 applies here.

DISCUSS

Offer a considered review of ethical considerations of studies related to promoting health. Conclusions should be presented clearly and supported by appropriate evidence.

Psychology of human relationships

10. Discuss the role of communication in maintaining relationships.　　　　[22]

Explain all terms which you use in your answer.

At least **two** empirical studies should be used in your answer.

Relevant studies and/or theories related to the role of communication in maintaining human relationships may include, but are not limited to:

- the importance of self-disclosure (Altman and Taylor's social penetration theory, 1973)
- the role of micro-expressions (Gottman and Levinson, 1986)
- relationship maintenance through communication (Canary and Dainton, 2003)
- marital type and communication (Weigel and Ballard-Reisch, 1999)
- attributional styles (Bradbury and Fincham, 1990)
- gender-based communication styles (Tannen, 1990).

Discussion may focus on:

- cultural biases in research
- methodological considerations
- gender differences in communication
- difficulties of carrying out research on communication styles
- ethical concerns when conducting research
- application of research to enhance positive communication in relationships.

AO3 applies here.

DISCUSS

This requires you to offer a considered review of the role of communication in maintaining relationships. Conclusions should be presented clearly and supported by appropriate evidence.

Psychology of human relationships

11. Evaluate research methods in the study of group dynamics. **[22]**

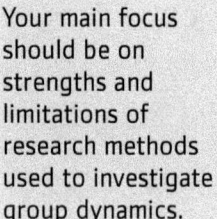

Explain all terms which will be used in your answer.

At least **two** empirical studies should be used in your answer.

ANSWER ANALYSIS

Your main focus should be on strengths and limitations of research methods used to investigate group dynamics.

AO3 applies here.

EVALUATE

This requires you to show critical analysis of research methods applied in empirical studies in the area of group dynamics. Conclusions should be presented clearly and supported by appropriate evidence.

Possible relevant research includes the following.

Experiments:
- Sherif et al. (1954)
- Kerr (1983)
- Phelps (2002)

Questionnaires (correlational):
- Croucher (2013)
- Novotny and Polansky (2011)

Correlational study:
- Stotts et al. (2001)

Focus group interview:
- Howarth (2002).

Psychology of human relationships

12. Evaluate research on bystanderism. [22]

The major focus of your answer should be on an evaluation of research, rather than a descriptive overview of the factors that influence bystanderism.

AO3 applies here.

EVALUATE

Make an appraisal of research (relevant studies) related to bystanderism by weighing up strengths and limitations of the research. Although a discussion of both strengths and limitations is required, it does not have to be evenly balanced to gain high marks.

Paper 3: Higher Level

- Set your timer for **1 hour**
- There are 24 marks available
- Answer **all** the questions

The stimulus material below is based on a study of cognitive dissonance.

Leon Festinger performed a classic study in 1956 with the aim to investigate a cognitive dissonance theory. He became a member of a small UFO cult (the seekers), members of which believed that an apocalypse is near and inevitable. Members of the cult
5 would be rescued as only true believers. Researchers (psychology students and employees) were trained for a month before the study started. To gain access to the cult, researchers made up some stories to convince true believers of their truthfulness. Four researchers (2 men and 2 women) took part in this investigation.
10 The main interest was put on how sure and committed people were to their beliefs. Members of this cult didn't have any schedule of meetings/activities, they were informed about meetings not long before, also they didn't live there on regular basis, also it was not possible to be left alone in the house. The study was conducted
15 between 19th November and 7th January. In the end, it turned out that no apocalypse happened, and the explanation of this shocking discovery was that the cult saved the world because of their true devotion.

[Source: Festinger, L, Riecken, H. W, Schachter, S. (1956), When Prophecy Fails: A Social and Psychological Study of a Modern Group that Predicted the Destruction of the World. Minneapolis: University of Minnesota Press]

Answer **all** of the following three questions, referring to the stimulus material in your answer. Marks will be awarded for demonstration of knowledge and understanding of research methodology.

1a. Identify the method used and outline **two** characteristics of the method. **[3]**

....
....
....
....
....
....
....
....
....
....
....
....
....
....
....
....

Before actually writing, try to prepare a very brief plan of every answer. You can use bullet points.

ANSWER ANALYSIS

Your answer should focus on research methods used in the stimulus material.

Remember not to give more than two characteristics of the method as you will not be given additional credit for it.

The characteristics of the method you identified could help you in differentiation between the one used in the study and other similar methods.

You should be very clear when identifying a research method: general terms will not be sufficient.

IDENTIFY

This question requires you to state the research method used in the study, as well as very briefly describe two characteristics of this method.

AO1 applies here.

1b. Describe the sampling method used in the study. [3]

Remember to analyse the text. Don't make a mistake in sampling method identification.

You need to describe how exactly the sampling method was implemented.

A sampling method can be used again when discussing the idea of generalization.

You should be careful not to focus on a research method instead of a sampling method.

AO1 applies here.

1c. Suggest an alternative or additional research method, giving **one** reason for your choice. [3]

ANSWER ANALYSIS

This answer should focus on one additional or alternative research method.

Remember not to give more than one reason of your choice as you will not be given additional credit for your answer.

You should be very clear when identifying possible research methods. General terms will not be sufficient.

AO2 applies here.

After identifying the research method used in the stimulus material, analyse strengths and limitations of this method. Focus on the most important ones as this will lead you to the choice of the most suitable additional/alternative method.

SUGGEST

Propose different research methods or additions to the given one. You also should explain your choice of research method.

2. Describe the ethical considerations that were applied in the study and explain if further ethical considerations could be applied. [6]

DESCRIBE

Give a detailed account of existing ethical issues and provide reasons for additional ethical considerations.

ANSWER ANALYSIS

You should focus on both aspects of ethical considerations to be awarded full marks.

ANSWER ANALYSIS

You could focus on informed consent, protection from harm, anonymity/ confidentiality, right to withdraw, deception and debriefing.

Remember to divide your answer into two paragraphs: one for ethical considerations applied in the study and another one for additional ones.

AO1 and AO2 apply here.

Be careful not to **overdo** one aspect of your answer (applied or additional ethical considerations).

3. Discuss how the researcher in the study could avoid bias. [9]

ANSWER ANALYSIS

You should focus on possible problems/ considerations that influence the outcomes or conclusions of research.

Remember to refer to specific biases in your answer.

When answering questions remember to refer to stimulus material as this will make your answer more valid.

Be careful not to only describe possible biases, but to focus on the ways to prevent them.

AO3 applies here.

DISCUSS

Present a balanced review of the possible ways to avoid biases in the given study.

Set C

This set of papers has no additional help in the margins. There is a space to write notes so you can plan what you are going to write if needed.

Paper 1: Standard Level and Higher Level

- Set your timer for **2 hours**
- There are 49 marks available
- Answer ALL the questions

Section A

Answer all **three** questions in this section. Marks will be awarded for focused answers demonstrating accurate knowledge and understanding of research.

Biological approach to understanding behaviour

1. Explain how **one** hormone may influence one human behaviour.   **[9]**

NOTES

Cognitive approach to understanding behaviour

2. Explain **one** study related to schema theory.   [9]

Sociocultural approach to understanding behaviour

3. With reference to a study investigating acculturation, outline **one** strength and **one** limitation of a research method used in the study. [9]

Section B

Answer **one** question in this section. Marks will be awarded for demonstration of knowledge and understanding (which requires the use of relevant psychological research), evidence of critical thinking (for example, application, analysis, synthesis, evaluation), and organization of answers.

4. Discuss the role of genes in **one** behaviour. [22]

5. Evaluate research on the influence of emotion on one cognitive process. [22]

6. Discuss stereotypes. [22]

NOTES

NOTES

NOTES

NOTES

Paper 2: Standard Level and Higher Level

SL:
- Set your timer for **1 hour**
- There are 22 marks available
- Answer **one** question

HL:
- Set your timer for **2 hours**
- There are 44 marks available
- Answer **two** questions (from different options)

NOTES

Abnormal psychology

1. Discuss the validity and/or reliability of diagnosis.   [22]

2. Discuss ethical considerations in the study of aetiologies of abnormal psychology.   [22]

3. Discuss the role of culture in the treatment of **one or more** disorders.   [22]

Developmental psychology

4. Discuss research methods in the study of developing as a learner.   [22]

5. Discuss the role of peers and/or play on cognitive and/or social development.
                                                                                    [22]

6. Discuss the development of empathy and/or theory of mind.   [22]

Health psychology

7. Discuss dispositional factors as determinants of health.   [22]

8. Discuss prevalence rates of **one** health problem.   [22]

9. Contrast research methods in the study of health promotion.   [22]

Psychology of human relationships

10. Evaluate research on explanations for why relationships change or end.   [22]

11. Discuss prejudice and/or discrimination.   [22]

12. Evaluate a biological approach to social responsibility.   [22]

NOTES

NOTES

NOTES

NOTES

NOTES

NOTES

Paper 3: Higher Level

- Set your timer for **1 hour**
- There are 24 marks available
- Answer **all** the questions

The stimulus material below is based on a study of post-traumatic stress disorder (PTSD).

Fieldman & Vengrober performed a qualitative research with the aim to investigate the symptoms of PTSD. Participants were 232 1.5 to 5 years of age children and their mothers, 148 of which were living near the Gaza Strip and as a result were exposed to war-related
5 trauma on everyday basis. 84 participants were controls living in Tel-Aviv (the area which was not exposed to war-related trauma). Participants received vouchers worth 80$ for taking part in the study and were approached through clinicians living in the area who were familiar with the clinical and childcare services for this
10 age. Participants helped to identify eligible friends and neighbors. The study took place during 2 years period of continuous rocket and missile attacks. Visits were not conducted on the day of the attack or in the next 3 days. Trained psychologists visited families at homes at least one month after attacks began and interviewed
15 children's mothers. Questions asked focused on the degree of exposure to war-trauma, child's emotional reactions, proximity to the explosion, potential injuries as well as potential expression of fear or horror. Some questions were also asked about possible developmental regression. Mothers were also asked to rate their
20 children's symptoms on a scale. Mothers in the control group were interviewed in the same way. The results showed that PTSD was diagnosed in 38% of children in the study, none of the kids in the control group were diagnosed with PTSD. Some children were resilient, however, being exposed to the same situations. There
25 was a difference in the number of children suffering from PTSD between toddlers and pre-schoolers (26% vs 45%).

[Source: Feldman, R and Vengrober, A. (2011), "Posttraumatic Stress Disorder in Infants and Young Children Exposed to War-Related Trauma", *Journal of the American Academy of Child & Adolescent Psychiatry*, Volume 50, Issue 7, pp. 645–656]

Answer **all** of the following three questions, referring to the stimulus material in your answer. Marks will be awarded for demonstration of knowledge and understanding of research methodology.

1a. Identify the method used and outline **two** characteristics of the method. **[3]**

1b. Describe the sampling method used in the study. [3]

_____

_____

_____

_____

_____

_____

_____

_____

1c. Suggest an alternative or additional research method giving **one** reason
for your choice. [3]

_____

_____

_____

_____

_____

_____

_____

_____

_____

2. Describe the ethical considerations in reporting the results and explain ethical
considerations that could be taken into account when applying the findings of
the study. [6]

_____

_____

_____

_____

_____

_____

_____

_____

_____

_____

_____

_____

_____

3. Discuss how a researcher could ensure that the results of the study are credible.

[9]

NOTES

Answers

Set A: Paper 1 (SL and HL): Section A

1. • **Neural networks** are networks of neurons connected by synapses to carry out electric impulses.
   • **Brain plasticity** (the ability of the brain to adjust its structure as a result of new/repeated experiences) serves as a base for neural networks formation.
   • As neurons are stimulated, electric signal is passed on from synapse to synapse. When neurons are repeatedly stimulated they become stronger and as a result new dendrites are built (this phenomenon is called dendritic branching) and more synapses are ready to be activated.
   • **Draganski (2004):** This showed that by learning new motor skills there will be changes in the brain structure (in this case, the behaviour was juggling). Significantly more grey matter in the mid-temporal areas was shown in juggling group in comparison with no jugglers; this clearly shows formation of neural networks as new connections between neurons were created because of performed activity.
   • **Maguire (2000).** This study focused on the role of experience and its effect on the structure of hippocampus, which is responsible for spatial memory. London taxi drivers were examined and the results showed a significant difference in density of posterior hippocampus (more grey matter in this area). This illustrates the formation of neural networks within hippocampus in response to repeated activity.

2. • **Multistore Memory Model** illustrates memory as three stores (stages). The information is transferred from one store to another.
   • MSM consists of: sensory memory, short-term memory (STM) and long-term memory (LTM); each of these components is different in terms of duration and capacity.
   • **Sensory memory** gathers everything that our senses are ready to focus on. This information is kept for a couple of seconds, depending on modality.
   • **Short-term memory** information is kept for no longer than 30 seconds; if rehearsed the duration is longer and eventually can be transferred to long-term memory. 7+/-2 is the Magic Number: this is how many pieces of information could be kept in STM (numbers, letters).
   • **Long-term memory**: capacity and duration are not explicitly identified as they are both potentially unlimited.
   • **Glanzer & Cunitz (1966):** This investigated primacy/recency effect. It means that one has a tendency to remember first and last pieces of information better than ones in the middle. The results of the study showed that in a condition with free recall, a task (filler task) made the recency effect disappear but primacy effect was intact. This supports the MSM theory and identifies STM and LTM as two separate memory stores.
   • **Milner (1966):** This involved Patient HM who suffered from epileptic seizures. He underwent a surgery for removal of the hippocampus. This part of the brain is said to be responsible for transferring information from STM to LTM. HM suffered from anterograde and had problems with encoding and retrieval; he couldn't form new memories. His working memory was intact as he was able to carry out normal conversation. He was also able to recall information from before surgery. It suggests that STM and LTM are two separate memory stores.

3. • **Culture** is defined by Matsumoto and Juang (2004) as a dynamic system of rules, explicit and implicit, established by groups to ensure their survival, involving attitudes, values, beliefs, norms and behaviours.
   • **Cultural norms** are the patterns of behaviour (attitudes and beliefs) that are characteristic of specific groups (cultures).
   • **Acculturation** is the psychological adjustment that occurs when two cultures come in direct contact with each other.
   • **Enculturation** is adopting or internalizing the schemas of your culture.
   • **Wang and Mallinckrodt (2006):** This explores how degrees of acculturation can lead to acculturative stress in Chinese and Taiwanese students, and how it is related to the cultural norms that they have been familiar with. Researchers used a survey and asked 104 students about their attitudes towards their original culture and their new foreign culture. The findings were that those who were able to maintain their original identity and adapt themselves to new culture experienced low acculturative stress, but those participants who experience attachment issues within new culture developed more severe acculturative stress. The study illustrates how the shift between cultures can affect people's social skills (behaviour).
   • **Ibañez (2015):** This was a study conducted with the aim of finding how the acculturative stress that Latino participants experienced when moving from their home countries to the United States impacted their relationships with their family. Researchers interviewed about 500 Latino participants. Findings suggest familial relationships deteriorated over time after moving to US; however, those experiencing more acculturative stress had better relationships with their families. Some cultures tend to reject cultural norms of their new culture and prefer to stick to their original culture (strong familial bonds). This study clearly shows how culture and cultural norms affect human behaviour by the effect enculturation has on human relationships.

Set A: Paper 1 (SL and HL): Section B
4. **(SL option)**
   • Pheromones are chemicals released to the environment by a member of one species and received by another individual of the same species. These substances have no smell, and their role in humans remains uncertain since adults have no functioning vomeronasal organ, which processes pheromone signals in animals. Most pheromones are responsible for sexual behavior and attractiveness.
   • **Wedekind et al. (1995)** conducted a study on the effects of pheromones on adults. 44 male students were asked to wear the same T-shirt for two nights in a row. The T-shirt was kept in a plastic bag between the two nights. Men were asked to keep the smell as neutral as possible by avoiding sexual activity, not smoking, not eating spicy food and not using perfumed products and products that produced a strong smell. After two nights, 49 female students were asked to rate six T-shirts for pleasure and fragrance intensity. Prior to the study, all male and female participants were classified for similarity to the immune systems (Major Histocompatibility Complex). Researchers discovered that women consistently prefer the smell of men whose immune system differs from their own (MHC dissimilar men), but only when they do not use birth control pills. The reason of this could be the fact that the more dissimilar the immune system the bigger chances of survival of future offspring. These results suggest that sweat contains pheromones or pheromones that may affect mate preferences.
   • **Roberts et al. (2008)** checked Wedekind's findings and investigated if taking birth control pills changes in smell preferences. The procedure for male participants reflected the procedure of Wedekind et al. and all participants performed blood tests to assess the similarity of the immune system. However, the study used an elongated design in which women were divided into two groups. The first group of women was examined before and after using the contraceptive pill, while the second group of women was a control group (without birth control pills) but attended test sessions at comparable intervals than the group using the contraceptive pills. The results confirmed the discoveries of Wedekind et al., there was a significant change in preferences towards the similarity of pheromones between men and women associated with the use of tablets, which was not visible in the control group.

The discussion may include, but is not limited to:
   • the effect of pheromones depends on the social and psychological context;
   • pheromones seem to influence behavior by changing the mental state, not by triggering fixed responses;
   • pheromones affect men and women differently;
   • methodological and ethical considerations, including ambiguity of empirical evidence;
   • application of results, including evidence for/against the role of vomeronasal organ and smell;
   • many studies on animals can't be generalized to humans;

117

- many studies show contradictory results and are difficult to replicate;
- there is a possibility of confounding variables which could affect the results.

4. (HL option)

- There are different reasons for using animals in a biological approach:
  - similar to humans in terms of physiology
  - easily accessible
  - shorter lifespans
  - some of the studies done on animals would be unethical to perform on human beings.
- Ethical considerations are controlled by the American Psychological Association, as well as the British Psychological Society (BPS). Every animal study needs to be approved by an ethics committee. BPS created 3Rs (replacement, reduction and refinement), which need to be taken under consideration at all times.
- Two of the most important ethical aspects in animal research are:
  - physical harm/inflicting pain (which refers to research designs)
  - justified choice (the reasons of choosing animals as subjects).
- **Rogers & Kesner (2003):** This laboratory experiment on rats studied acetylcholine levels on memory. Researchers tested two groups of rats that had learned a route of a maze and were later injected with either a saline solution (a placebo) or scopolamine (which blocks acetylcholine receptor sites). The group of rats with a decrease in acetylcholine levels made more errors and therefore were slower than the group that was injected with a saline solution. This led to the conclusion that having a decrease in acetylcholine resulted in less-effective recall of the maze.
  - The study was not ethical, because a large group of rats were harmed through injecting chemicals that changed their memory, which suggests a high extent of suffering after the research was completed. The researchers used an invasive technique by injecting chemicals into the hippocampus. This can suggest inflicting pain or harm.
  - The choice of animals for this study needs to be clearly justified in terms of scientific purpose (if it does increase the knowledge or benefit humans), for example in terms of physiological similarities between rats and humans.
- **Merzenich et al. (1984):** This study investigated neuroplasticity, more specifically cortical representation of the hand in eight adult owl monkeys. Hand digits were mapped in the cortex. Then the third digit (the middle finger) was amputated. After two months, remapping was done to see changes in the cortex. Researchers found that adjacent areas (digits two and four) spread and started using the area which has belonged to digit three before amputation. This study clearly shows neuroplasticity of the brain.
  - This study has some serious ethical considerations. An invasive technique was used which had irreversible effect (finger amputation) and inflicting pain and physical harm was possible after the surgery (however, it is worth noting that the monkeys were anesthetized before the amputation).
  - Justification of the study in terms of cortical mapping in humans and the increase of the knowledge about the brain should be discussed as an argument.
- **All ethical issues should be discussed as well:**
  - Prior knowledge of particular species would help with proper treatment.
  - Only the minimum number of animals should be used.
  - Distress, discomfort, pain should be minimized at all times.
- There should also be some basic discussion about the value of animal research and the justification of its use.

5.
- **Reliability of memory** – the extent to which our memories are direct records of what happened in real life or distorted by uncontrolled factors.
- Reconstructive memory means that memory is not static. It is instead an active process that is influenced by many factors (such as post-event information) every time we remember or recall something.
- One of the most important theories concerned about the topic of human memory is Bartlett's schema theory. This suggests the schema is 'unconscious mental structures, that represent an individual's generic knowledge about the world. It is through schemata that old knowledge influences new information' (William F. Brewer, 'Learning Theory – Schema Theory'). This also explains the way reconstructive memories work. According to Bartlett, memory of an event is affected by previous knowledge, experience, origin (cultural background) and personal views.

Hence, information which is unknown or missing is exchanged and filled by the familiar schema.
- **Loftus & Palmer (1974):** The aim of this study was to investigate how post-event information (leading questions) affects the memory of a witness for that event and hence prove that eye-witnesses are not completely reliable. The participants were shown a short clip (30 seconds) of a car crash. Afterwards, they were asked to provide answers for a questionnaire. A question was 'How fast were the cars going when they "smashed"/"collided"/"bumped"/"contacted"/"hit" each other?'. Each group was given a different word, chosen from the ones listed above. The outcome was that the estimated speed when the words 'smashed' and 'collided' occurred was significantly higher (40.8 and 39.3 mph) than when the words with lighter association were used. The researchers concluded that the intensity of the word used and the attitude towards it affects the height of the speed suggested by participants.
- **Yuille & Cutshall (1986):** The aim of this study was identical with Loftus & Palmer; however, the study was done in a natural environment and made use of a naturally occurring event. Researchers criticized the schema theory and conducted research aiming to evaluate the accuracy of witness accounts. The research showed that the misleading questions had not affected the memories being recalled but, on the contrary, they were quite vivid and accurate. Although this experiment may have refuted Loftus and Palmer's findings to some extent, it brought up crucial issues of the eyewitness testimony's reliability.
  - Researchers used the field experiment as a research method, so this study has high ecological validity.
  - It was a one-time natural situation so would be impossible to replicate.
  - Experimenters admitted that the results of the study could be due to a different phenomenon: **flashbulb memory**.
- Human memory is highly reconstructive and can be subjective. What's more, the way we produce memories is influenced by schemas. Human brains transform and reconstruct processed images into memories in such a way that they are coherent with already existing schemas. However, reconstructive memory is a phenomenon that is found in experimental conditions, not in the natural environment, according to studies given in this answer.

6.
- **Social cognitive theory** is based on observational learning. This means that humans tend to learn as a result of observing the environment and, most importantly, other humans. It is often applied to developmental psychology, due to the fact that children and adolescents are constantly surrounded by role models, all of whom exhibit behaviour that might create an influence. Other important factors in social cognitive theory are: self-efficacy (am I capable of mastering observed behaviour?), identification with the model and reciprocal determinism (three different factors: personal, behavioural and environmental, which affect each other in bidirectional ways).
- **Bandura, Ross & Ross (1961):** The aim of this experiment was to see if children would exhibit more aggressive behaviour if they were exposed to a similarly aggressive role model, and whether the gender of the role model would affect the child differently. The sample consisted of 72 children, 36 boys and 36 girls. They were divided into three groups, with the first 24 (12 boys and 12 girls) used as the control. The other group was split to have 6 boys and 6 girls watching an aggressive male model, and 6 boys and 6 girls watching a female aggressive model. The same was done with the third group, but a non-aggressive role model was used. So half the children saw a same-sex role model, and the other saw an opposite-sex role model. The children were then placed in a room that contained toys (including the Bobo doll) and allowed to play. The results showed that the group that had watched the aggressive role model imitated their aggressive behaviour more often than the two other groups. The same sex imitation happened more often in boys than girls. Boys also exhibited more physically aggressive behaviour on average than the girls, whereas the girls inflicted a higher amount of verbal aggression. The study concluded that the results support the social cognitive theory, demonstrating how children learn behaviour by imitating the behaviour of those they see. It supports the social cognitive theory's assumption that behaviour is based on that of a group's other members, and that it is learned through observing another's behaviour.
  - **Strengths:** Bandura used matched-pairs design, which helped with confounding variables (internal difference in aggression between children). The study is also easily replicable given

the laboratory setting. The study was a strong demonstration of the basis of the social cognitive theory, helping to further research in this area of psychology;

- **Limitations:** The fact that it was a laboratory study resulted in low-ecological validity, given the unrealistic scenarios used to test for aggression. The model and child did not personally interact and the model was a complete stranger, which is unrealistic since most children's role models are family and close friends. The ethics of the experiment are questionable as there could have been long-term consequences for children viewing such aggressive behaviours. Furthermore, demand characteristics could be present since the children could have acted aggressively on purpose, thinking that this was what the researchers wanted. The sample was very small so it's impossible to generalize findings to a larger population. The study has low temporal validity as it was done in 1960s.

- **Konijn et al (2007) I Wish I Were a Warrior study:** Researchers wanted to find out if violent video games are particularly likely to increase aggression when players identify with violent game characters. The sample consisted of 112 teenage boys from the Netherlands, all of whom did not possess much educational ability. This was intentional because they would be more likely to consume violent images as compared to boys with higher educational ability. They were randomly assigned to play either a realistic violent game, a non-realistic violent game, a realistic non-violent game, or a non-realistic non-violent game. After they had played a game for 20 minutes, they were paired with an ostensible partner to play a game where their reaction time was tested. The boys were told that the participant that responded the slowest would have a loud noise played on their headphones (which was the aggression measure), and the participant that won that round would get to choose the decibel of the noise. They were informed that the higher volumes could cause permanent hearing damage. After the game was finished, the boys filled out a form where they assessed their level of wishful identification (with a character in a game), how realistic they thought the game was, and how immersed they were with the content. The results showed that the most aggressive participants were the boys that had played the realistic aggressive video game and expressed a high level of wishful identification with the character. They used the loudest noise levels on the ostensible partner, even though they were unprovoked. The study concluded that people who wishfully identify with a violent video game character are likely to be more aggressive, especially if the video game is realistic in nature and the player themselves feel immersed. The study is pivotal in understanding how even behaviour from fictional characters can be mimicked by people in reality, and that the social cognitive theory is not limited to people that a person interacts with, but rather even fictional characters or media personalities. The study is able to connect the social cognitive theory to today's technology-led world, and show the negative effects of our digital progress.

  - **Limitations**: The sampling method consisted of only Dutch adolescent boys, limiting its generalizability to only one gender and one age group. The sample was also of boys of low-education ability. Future research may compare male and female participants of different ages and educational ability levels. The amount of time the boys spent actually playing the game was another limitation; it can be argued that just a 20-minute exposure develops only a surface-level understanding of a game and character, which would distort how a teenager views the video game and character. The same can be said about the narratives of the video game, which can transform a character as the gameplay moves forward.

  - **Strengths**: No immediate ethical considerations since the participants played video games that are mainstays in video game culture and appropriate for viewing. The realistic nature of the video games also mimicked real life, making the applicability of the study to real life much more authentic. The study reflected the social cognitive theory's effects in today's digital advanced world, and how our digital native society is changing the way we internalise information and actions during our developing years.

- Some general issues with research into social cognitive theory are that other factors are not taken under consideration (such as biological factors) or the fact that some studies were natural experiments, meaning confounding variables can potentially affect the study. Some studies are also correlational so no cause and effect can be established, which also raises the question about bidirectional ambiguity.

Set A: Paper 2 (SL and HL)

1. • Psychological diagnosis refers to observable symptoms (emotional, cognitive or behavioural) which don't have an organic base, as well as self-reported description of a patient.

   • **Confirmation bias** is defined as the disposition that researchers have when gathering information to confirm and validate what they already believe. This can lead to researchers unintentionally favouring evidence that confirms their assumptions and tending to leave evidence that does not support their initial opinion unnoticed. Additionally, evidence can be interpreted to better fit the researcher's beliefs, rather than being attributed to another explanation or interpreted to confirm another argument.

   • **Reporting bias** is defined as the difference between the cases reported in studies and hospital admission and the real-life prevalence of the illness. This is common in cultures where it is not common to seek help from a mental health professional, or in the case of an illness that can very easily be categorised as another (either due to a lack of knowledge or the lack of distinct symptoms). In some cases, cultural taboos or limitations can also affect the reporting of the illnesses, which causes the reporting bias.

   • **Mendel et al. (2011):** This study aimed to research the process of diagnosis in order to see how mental health professionals can be dispositioned to have confirmation bias. The 2011 study provided 75 psychiatrists and 75 medical students with a decision task, and were asked to research for new information after having made a diagnosis. The study found that 13% of the psychiatrists and 25% of the medical students exhibited a confirmation bias when they were searching for new information. Most participants were less likely to change their first diagnosis after they searched for evidence that supported their early diagnosis than those who had searched for information that did not support the original diagnosis. The psychiatrists who were looking for confirmatory research had made an incorrect diagnosis about 70% of the time. Furthermore, the participants of the study that chose an incorrect diagnosis prescribed incorrect treatment options when compared to participants with the correct diagnosis. This could cause injury and/or irreversible harm to patients in extreme cases. Researchers concluded that a confirmatory information search has higher chances of leading to an incorrect diagnosis, which is why psychiatrists should be conscious of the confirmation bias and use techniques that could help to reduce it.

   • **Angel and Thoits (1987):** This study demonstrated how cognitive interpretations of symptoms differentiate between cultures, and how this affects the reporting and diagnosis of mental illnesses and disorders. The example used in this study is of the under-reporting of certain mental disorders in Mexico. Researchers described the stages in which the illness develops, and how reporting bias occurs in the last two stages (which include labelling and action). After the symptoms are compared against those of the home culture, and if the symptoms carry a negative association which is a stigma, patients are less likely to report their condition or seek help from a mental health professional. Researchers found that this was prevalent in Mexico, where patients are more likely to seek treatment in the forms of traditional medicine, such as herbal medicine. This lack of reporting results in a skewed statistic and an incorrect form of diagnosis and treatment, which in the end are most harmful for those who are mentally ill.

   Discussion of biases plus evaluation of studies:

   • As the studies illustrate and describe, clinical biases often have exclusively negative effects in the diagnosis of mental disorders. The confirmation bias and reporting bias often work in tandem, along with cultural taboos and under-reporting of mental illness to result in an incorrect diagnosis. Mendel et al.'s study demonstrates the undoing ways in which psychiatrists are prone to the confirmation bias, and shows how it can be enhanced when only looking into confirmatory information.

   • **Angel and Thoits (1987):** A similar issue arises with this study, since the researchers only used one case study to illustrate the reporting bias. It does not account for a stereotypically 'repressive' culture, or one that has culture-bound syndromes (a misdiagnosis that arrives from an abnormal behaviour that only exists within one culture, which would not be able to result in a correct diagnosis if treated by a mental health professional outside that particular culture). The prevalence of reporting bias is higher in those cultures.

   • Clinical biases play a defining role in diagnosis, and often only have a negative impact on those who are affected by a mental illness. Not only is it the incorrect diagnosis, but rather the lack of diagnosis in a few cases. The confirmation bias and reporting bias are two examples of clinical biases that hinder the diagnosis of mental illnesses, and need to be better researched to be avoided during diagnosis.

2. • Major depressive disorder (MDD) is diagnosed when a person experiences at least two weeks of depressed mood or loss of interest and pleasure. An additional four symptoms should also be diagnosed.
 • Three main factors are taken under consideration in terms of reasons for this disorder: biological (genetics, neurobiology), cognitive and sociocultural.
 • Genetics and/or serotonin hypothesis and/or cortisol hypothesis can be used as a biological approach to aetiology of MDD.
 • **Caspi et al. (2003):** People who had short versions of the five HTT allele showed more symptoms of depression in response to stressful life events. The effect was strongest for those with more stressful life events. Inheriting the gene was not enough to lead to depression, but if people experienced some stressful life situations it increased the likelihood of developing depression.
 • Some points in discussion could include the correlational nature of this study. The fact that some people with depression do not have the shorter version of this five HTT allele should also be explained.
 • **Kendler (2006):** The rate of depression inheritance was assessed by interviews according to modified DSM-IV criteria in 42,161 twins, including 15,003 pairs, from the Swedish national twin register. The results indicate that the inheritance rate for major depression was significantly higher in women (42%) than in men (29%), and the genetic risk factors for major depression were moderately correlated in men and women. The results were higher in MZ (monozygotic) than DZ (dizygotic) twins. This study suggests that heredity of major depression is higher in women than in men, and that some genetic risk factors for major depression are gender dependent.
 • **Critical thinking** – sociocultural factors were not taken under consideration, meaning that Nolen-Hoeksema's theory can be used as a counter argument in this discussion (cognitive argument).
 • **Discussion** could also point out that there are other cultural influences that can't be controlled, so the exact role of these factors is unknown. Twins are a very small population, so as a result the findings of this sort of study don't necessarily represent the phenomenon in the society.

3. • Major depressive disorder (MDD) is diagnosed when a person experiences at least two weeks of depressed mood or loss of interest and pleasure. An additional four symptoms should also be diagnosed.
 • There are **two approaches to treatment** in general: biological, which assumes that if there is a biological cause there also needs to be biological solution (such as drug therapy); and psychological, which uses different kinds of psychotherapies (individual or group). The aim of latter is to get to the roots of the problem by analysing thoughts and behaviours of a patient.
 • **CBT** stands for cognitive behavioural therapy. It is based on Beck's cognitive theory, which says that automatic negative thoughts lead to irrational behaviour. This therapy deals with thoughts by restructuring them. It also aims to change unhealthy behavioural patterns by the subject learning how to deal with problematic situations (developing coping strategies).
 • **Elkin (1989):** Researchers compared interpersonal therapy (IPT) and CBT of patients suffering from MDD. 250 people took part in this study and were randomly assigned to 1 of 4 16-week treatment conditions: IPT, CBT, medication plus clinical help, and placebo with clinical help. Patients in every group showed significant difference in terms of reduction of symptoms. Researchers claimed that there was a limited evidence for the specific effectiveness of IPT and CBT.
 • **DeRubeis (2005):** This study used the experience of competent clinicians from the University of Pennsylvania. It aimed to compare the efficacy in moderate to severe depression of antidepressant medications with cognitive therapy in a placebo-controlled trial. 240 patients, aged 18 to 70 years, with moderate to severe major depressive disorder took part in the study. After eight weeks the response rate in the medication (50%) and CBT (43%) groups was higher than in the placebo group (25%). Analysis based on continuous results after eight weeks showed an advantage for each of the therapies in comparison to placebo,

each with a medium-sized effect. The benefit was significant for drugs compared to the placebo and at the level of a negligible trend in cognitive therapy compared to placebo. After 16 weeks, the response rates were 58% in each of the conditions; remission rates were 46% for drugs, 40% for cognitive therapy.
 • **Arguments in discussion** can also consider relapse rates and the study by **Rush et al. (March 1977)**. Participants were randomly assigned to individual treatment with either cognitive therapy or medication (imipramine). Both treatments lasted for 12 weeks. Both treatment groups showed statistically significant decreases in depressive symptomatology. Cognitive therapy resulted in significantly greater improvement than pharmacotherapy on both a self-administered measure of depression. 79% of the patients in cognitive therapy showed marked improvement or complete remission of symptoms as compared to 23% of the pharmacotherapy patients.
 • **Other arguments:** There are no side effects in CBT therapy compared to drug therapy. Furthermore, CBT teaches patients how to deal with problems rather than just masking symptoms. On the other hand, there are some dangerous situations (such as suicidal thoughts) where patients cannot afford to be engaged in CBT – they need help in this specific moment, so drug therapy would be more effective. It is also unknown if cognitive distortions cause depression: they may simply be a symptom of depression.

4. • **Cognitive development** focuses on how cognitive processes (memory, thinking, decision making or perception) develop over time and how these changes affect our behaviour.
 • **Piaget** claimed that knowledge is gained through mental representations known as schemas. These are changed throughout life and modified as a result of experience. This modification is called adaptation (assimilation and adaptation). Another claim was that children actively seek information by interaction with their external environment, which helps children to develop cognitively.
 • **Piaget** coined four sequential stages of cognitive development:
   – the sensorimotor stage (0–2 years) (no formal schema of any kind about the world or the child itself). The knowledge can be gained by direct interaction with the environment.
   – the pre-operational stage (2–7 years) (logical operations and object permanence dominate, children don't have a sense of conservation). The study made by Piaget and Inhelder (1956) used the three mountains task to demonstrate the egocentrism characteristic for this stage.
   – the concrete operational stage (7–11 years). Children develop rules and/or schemas of the world, and these rules can be used in real-situations and are called 'operations'.
   – the formal operational stage (from 11 years onwards). In this last stage, mental structures are very well developed, and ideas and problems can be analysed mentally without real objects.
 • **Some stages have been criticized:**
   – Testing the sensorimotor stage, **Bower (1982)** prepared an experiment which showed that the children showed enough surprise after the disappearance of an object to say that object permanence was more flexible than Piaget thought.
   – The concrete operational stage was criticized by **McGarrigle and Donaldson (1974)** as they questioned methods used by Piaget. They use a puppet which transformed beads. The results were that 63% of children were able to conserve a number as they recognized the number of beads remained the same. These results are contradictory of Piaget's theory.
 • **Strengths**: Piaget's theory was the first theory of cognitive development. The theory is based on determination and a constructivist approach, which perceives children as active thinkers. Piaget was the first to connect biological maturation with cognitive development and this notion is widely accepted and used nowadays. His assumption about constructivism is also widely recognized and accepted. It also significantly influenced education.
 • **Limitations**: Piaget's methods were widely criticized for being too formal for young children. He also didn't distinguish between competence and performance. Piaget didn't consider language as an important factor in cognitive development. His theory is also criticized for not focusing on real-life situations and social development (what was visible in his three-mountain-task study). His theory is overly descriptive; however, doesn't provide many explanations for the stages.

5. • Trauma, neglect and abuse have a serious effect on children's development. Many studies confirm the fact that there could be severe long-term consequences in terms of social and cognitive

development. However, as every human being is different, it's very difficult to predict these effects as we all react differently, and some of us develop resilience as well.

- **Rutter (2007):** This study was a long-term analysis on normal versus impaired functioning across seven domains. It was conducted on children who had experienced profound institutional deprivation up to the age of 42 months and were adopted from Romania into UK families. Comparisons were made with noninstitutionalized children adopted from Romania and with non-deprived within-UK adoptees placed before the age of 6 months. Specifically, the validity of the assessment, the degree of continuity and change in levels of functioning from 6 to 11 years, and the factors in the pre- and post-adoption environment accounting for heterogeneity in outcome were examined. Pervasive impairment was significantly raised in children experiencing institutional deprivation for 6 months or longer, with a minority within this group showing no impairment. There was no additional significant effect of duration of deprivation beyond the 6-month cut off, and few other predictors explained outcome.
- **Criticism:** This is a longitudinal study, so it was possible to observe changes which took place over time. Another important characteristic is the large sample that he used. It is not possible to determine how many children's behaviours are the result of other serious situations, such as malnutrition, deprivation or abuse.
- **Sun (2016):** Psychotic-like experiences (PLEs) are thought to be associated with childhood deprivation and may predict later psychotic disorders but have not been studied in this potentially vulnerable population. More 'left-behind' children were reported experiencing PLEs than others. They also scored higher on the overall frequency of PLEs, severity of childhood trauma, and the subjectively perceived psychological impact of trauma both at the time of the events and at present. Compared with 'left-behind' children raised by a parent or by grandparents, those raised by others reported suffering more severe impact both at the time of the events and at present.
- **Aversive childhood experiences** (ACEs) play a significant role in children's emotional, cognitive and social development. However, the problem with research in this area is that because every child and every trauma is different (for example, sexual abuse, emotional abuse or neglect) it is not possible to identify cause-and-effect relationship. Most of these studies are correlational in nature and definite conclusions can't be made.
- **Resilience:** The ability to withstand or recover quickly from difficult conditions and its biological roots should also be taken under consideration (medial prefrontal cortex, hippocampal pathways or 5-HT neurotransmitter).

6. • **Attachment** is a strong emotional relationship between two individuals. It has an evolutionary basis, as babies strongly attached to their mothers are more likely to survive and function better in a society and in future relationships. If children are separated from their mothers they react with stress, lack of comfort and anxiety.
- **Strange situation paradigm** involves observation of the child who is playing while parents and strangers enter and leave the room, creating some new and unfamiliar situations and mixing them with familiar ones.
- **Van Ijzendoorn & Kroonenberg (1988):** Nearly 2,000 classifications of Ainsworth strange situations were obtained in eight different countries. Differences and similarities between the distributions in the sample classifications were examined by correspondence analysis. Significant differences between cultures have been identified; in many cases, samples from one country more closely resembled samples from other countries than with each other. The data also suggests a pattern of intercultural differences, in which avoidance classifications appear as relatively more common in Western European countries, and resistant classifications as relatively more common in Israel and Japan. The intercultural difference was almost 1.5 times greater than the intercultural one.
- **Criticism:** Data is taken from individualistic developed countries.
  – The validity of the test is questionable. The paradigm is said to be overly focused on specific cultural dimensions.
  – Generalization of the findings for the whole culture could be difficult as the sample was relatively small.
  – Researcher bias could appear as studies for meta-analysis could be chosen to confirm researcher's preconceptions.
  – This study was conducted many years ago and so parenting styles and family structure could be different now (low temporal validity)

- **Hazan and Shaver (1987):** This study explores the theory that adult romantic attachment reflects a person's perception of early style of care. The conclusions were that the caregiver's warmth was positively correlated with a high, safe adult score. The caregiver's high uncertain outcome was positively correlated with the adult high attachment uncertainty. The implications for adult attachment theory were discussed, as were measurement limitations and other issues related to future research.
- However, researchers were cautious about drawing too many conclusions as it's not said that insecurely attached children will develop insecure relationships in adulthood. Volunteers were used, so people were more motivated than the majority of society would be. Sampling bias took place and more women took part in the study. Self-reports are also not the best way to gather information as these are highly subjective, answers can be biased because of the expectations participants could have towards the study. Most of studies into attachment are done in western individual societies. Also collectivistic should be investigated to draw more significant conclusions.
- **Research on attachment** is based on the assumption that there are some mental systems which activate emotional processes (emotional relationships). For many, it is an innate need which manifests itself in basic infant activities *(smiling, crying, etc.) This is why it is so hard to study this phenomenon and measure it, as every individual has different relationships with his/her caregiver. What's more, some classic studies were done many years ago (Bowlby's theory in 1951, and Ainsworth, Harlow in 1971) so we cannot generalize and apply those findings to present times.

7. • **Health beliefs** are internal preconceptions about health. These are stable cognitive schemas which are based on our previous experience; these mental representations help to understand situations and adjust behaviour accordingly. One of the principles of cognitive approach is that people's views are resistant to change; the same is true of health beliefs and so, although not always accurate, we tend to follow them.
- **Health belief model (HBM)** was presented in 1966 by Rosenstock. It is focused on the prediction of health behaviours and is based on opinions and attitudes of individuals. HBM follows two assumptions. The first is that humans think rationally so they can make accurate decisions that are best for them (so if there is a serious threat it is probably that a person will act accordingly to fight this threat). The second assumption is that we are all different, so we perceive the world and health-related situations differently. This attitude will affect our behaviour towards a potential decrease of health risk.
- **Weinberger et al. (1981):** This study gathered opinions and beliefs about smoking from 120 former and current smokers. It suggested that ex-smokers consider smoking to be a serious health problem. They did not report that the doctor advised them to stop smoking and personally felt susceptible to its negative effects. Moderate smokers also consider smoking to have serious consequences, but they do not consider themselves susceptible to its negative effects. The data suggests that some attitudes may affect health-related behaviours – in order to quit smoking it is not enough for the person to believe that smoking is a serious health problem: they also need to perceive themselves as prone to its negative effects.
- **Reed et al. (1999):** This study explored the negative expectations of HIV, AIDS-related mourning, and the interaction of expectations and mourning as predictors of significant HIV-related symptoms among previously asymptomatic HIV-infected gay men. 72 HIV-positive men with no symptoms since the start of the study were selected to take part in this study. Participants were investigated for two-and-a-half to three-and-a-half years after psychosocial assessment; their symptoms were assessed every 6 months. The interaction of negative expectations associated with HIV and mourning was an important predictor of the onset of symptoms. Negative expectations towards participants' health situation predicted the further development of symptoms in bereaved men controlling their immune status, high-risk sexual behaviour, substance use and major depression disorder.
- **Criticism:** Both studies included self-assessment, which is not a reliable source of information because of the highly subjective character of information; participants in this study are also susceptible to demand characteristics. No cause and effect is established as answers only illustrate trends. Samples in both studies were not big so it is difficult to generalize the findings to other populations. As studies are mostly correlational, HBM is also not well presented in terms of explanations of health-

related behaviours. Another argument in criticism is that it's just one side of argument; there are definitely other factors which influence our behaviours (cognitive, biological or sociocultural).

8. • **Stress** has been widely studied for many reasons. It affects our everyday life: we need to face stressors and cope with them to maintain our well-being. Most of research done is based on Hans Selye General Adaptation Syndrome, which assumes that every stressful situation needs to follow three stages (alarm reaction, resistance and exhaustion). Stress is a health problem as it affects our body functioning (increases levels of adrenaline, cortisol, affects our immune system and memory). However, it depends if stress is acute or mild and long-lasting, as both have different influences on our organism.

• **Kiecolt-Glaser et al. (1984):** The aim of this study was to check if exam stress affects our immune response. The participants were 75 medical students preparing for their exams; they were all volunteers. Researchers took blood samples one month before exams to identify the level of white cells (stress level). They were also asked about any life-changing situations that would raise their level of stress. After that they were divided into two groups: a **high-stress** and a **low-stress** group. After participants took their exams, second blood samples were taken to identify the activity of NK cells (responsible for high functioning immune system). Researchers noticed a significant decrease in NK cell activity between blood tests. Participants in the 'high-stress' group more often had lower NK levels than those in the 'low-stress' group. It clearly shows that the stress experienced before exams significantly affected the immune system's ability to cope with the stress of research.

  – This natural experiment is ethical as no psychological or physical harm was done to participants, informed consent was obtained, and no deception was used.

  – Participants of the study were young students who are used to examination stress. Students are also more available, willing and motivated to take part in psychological studies. So generalization of findings to other populations would be difficult.

  – The study was done in natural environment, so it has high ecological validity. However not all variables were controlled; we do not know if some participants were engaged in some coping strategies that would help them handle the examination stress, so this is a possible confounding variable.

  – Researchers use repeated measures design: they investigated the same group twice, as they measured their level of NK cells twice (before and after examinations). This meant it was possible to effectively compare these results. They also controlled participants variability.

  – Stress is also difficult to operationalize as every individual has different experience and perceives this phenomenon in different ways. It is impossible to identify objective situations (stressors) which would activate stress responses for every individual.

• The results of this study are supported by the study made by **Cohen (1991)**, which investigated whether chronic stress makes people more vulnerable to common colds. The results showed that the percentage of infection ranged from 74 to 90 percent in correlation with the level of mental stress.

  – There is an important argument in the discussion of ethics in this study, as people were exposed to viruses that can potentially have serious repercussions afterwards.

  – Reliable and valid studies in the area of health psychology should follow guidelines. They should consider long-term effects and be performed in natural habitat.

9. • WHO defines **health promotion** as the process of enabling people to increase control over, and to improve their health. Health promotion strategies aim to prevent illnesses and make sure that people are engaged in healthy habits. Despite these strategies, it's very difficult to convince people to behave in a healthy way. The reasons are both external and internal: our motivation, individual attitudes about certain activities, social and cultural differences, some gender differences, and knowledge about health and health problems.

• **Challenge!** This health promotion model focuses on obesity prevention and health promotion. It is based on social cognitive theory, modelling and mentorship. Each person is given a mentor who spends time with him/her. Each session is a different kind of challenge and participants also set themselves an individual goal to achieve (which might include eating habits, a physical

activity, etc.). The role of mentors is to sustain motivation and reformulate goals, as well as discuss progress, successes and failures. This programme is effective in BMI reduction; however, the results are visible after 24 months.

  – **Black et al. (2010):** The aim of this study was to investigate changes in BMI status, body composition, physical activity and diet during a 12-session health promotion/obesity prevention program: Challenge!

  – 235 black teenagers (aged 11–16; 38% overweight/obese) from low-income urban communities took part in the study. Participants were randomly assigned to health promotion/obesity prevention, which is anchored in social cognitive theory and motivational interviews, or were provided with school-age black mentors for control. Post-intervention assessments (11 months) and delayed assessments (24 months) were carried out.

  – Retention was 76% in 2 years. Overweight/obesity decreased by 5% among intervention youth and increased by 11% among the control youth. In overweight/obese adolescents, the intervention reduced the total percentage of body fat and fat mass and increased lean mass with a delayed observation period. It increased physical activity equivalent to playing after the intervention, but not with a delayed observation period. The intervention youth decreased significantly more in terms of snack/dessert consumption than the control youth during both follow-up assessments.

  – In the post-intervention period, the impact of the intervention on diet and PA was observed, but not on BMI category or body composition. With a delayed observation period, diet changes were maintained and intervention prevented the BMI category from rising. Body composition in overweight/obesity has been improved.

• Health campaigns are usually intended to cause fear, but their use is often ineffective in achieving the desired behaviour change. According to established learning principles, fear will most likely be effective if the campaign reduces the level of fear. In some circumstances, it may be difficult to meet these requirements. In general, a positive reinforcement approach may prove more effective than using fear.

• **THINK AGAIN Campaign** in Canada: The focus of this campaign was on parents of children aged 5–11 years. The campaign aimed to motivate parents, and in particular mothers, to get their children active by increasing parents' awareness that their children may not be active enough to meet the guidelines. It focused on increasing the awareness of parents regarding other children's physical activity levels, thus motivating them to take action to support their children to be more active. Advertisements had a key message, that children need at least 60 minutes of physical activity every day. These advertisements were aired on various types of media.

• **Berry et al. (2014):** This study conducted an experimental study to investigate mothers' intention to support children's physical activity after watching campaign ads, with an emphasis on determining the role of some cognitive variables such as credibility, agreement, commitment and attention to advertising in the campaign. The likelihood of elaboration (ELM) model was chosen as the theoretical model to determine whether indirect responses (i.e. unconscious responses without reflection time, such as implicit consent) and reflective responses (i.e. conscious responses such as explicit credibility and commitment) to message advertising might differentially predict cognition (i.e. attitudes, intentions) related to the behaviour promoted by the campaign. The mothers (N = 102) who took part in the study were asked to watch one of the 'Think Again' ads and fulfil the task of presumption of consent, followed by questionnaires. The results showed that mothers who noticed the message of the campaign and were concerned about the physical activity of their own children, more often led their children to greater physical activity. In addition, the results confirmed that there was a gap between the perception of mothers (implicit consent) and the reality regarding the level of physical activity of their children. Many mothers believed that their children had sufficient activity, but only a few reported that their children were active every day of the week.

• To effectively discuss health promotion strategies and their effectiveness, one needs to think about different factors: reliable and valid evaluation needs resources (time and money), and funding bias can play a role as people who lead specific programmes also take part in its evaluation (it may lead to researcher bias as well). The amount of data means it must be obtained using self-reported surveys/questionnaires (this source of information is highly subjective). The effectiveness of campaigns could be visible after long periods of time; however, confounding variables could also affect the results. Generalization could be problematic, as well as the number of people in the sample or sampling method (e.g. purposive sampling) because of sampling bias. In many cases with big campaigns, it is impossible to identify cause-and-effect relationships so researchers could draw conclusions only based on correlations and not causations.

10. • Biological factors in human relationships include evolutionary, genetic and neurochemical explanations. Each one influences us in a different way. Evolutionary theory focuses on the choice of the partner which potentially can provide for family and/or will give birth to healthy children. Genetic arguments claim that in line with evolution there is a biological compatibility in terms of interpersonal attraction. Finally neurochemical arguments focus on neurotransmitters (dopamine), hormones (oxytocin) or pheromones which affect our personal relationships.

  • **Wedekind (1995):** One significant benefit of sexual reproduction may be that it allows animals (including humans) to respond quickly to ever-changing selection pressure in the environment, such as co-occurring parasites. This would be most effective if the females were able to provide their offspring with certain combinations of alleles for the loci that could be crucial in the host-host arms race, for example MHC (major histocompatibility complex). The study shows that MHC affects both body odours and body odour preferences in humans, and women's preferences depend on their hormonal status. Female and male students have been enrolled in HLA-A, -B and -DR. Each student wore a shirt for two consecutive nights. The next day, each student was asked to assess the smell of six shirts. They rated men's body odour as more pleasant when they were different from men in MHC than when they were more similar. This difference in odour evaluation was reversed when women assessing odour took oral contraceptives. In addition, men's fragrances unlike MHC remind women more often of their own actual or former partners than those of men similar to MHC. This suggests that MHC or linked genes today affect partner selection.

  • There is an increasing amount of work which shows that the MHC may not only influence mate choice but also maternal selection thereafter. Findings show that some genetically determined odour components can be important in mate choice. However, there are some flaws. No additional factors were taken under considerations (sociocultural and/or cognitive) and the role of MHC from an evolutionary point of view is oversimplified.

  • **Buss (1989):** This study investigated cross-cultural similarities and differences in males/female mate preferences. Over 10,000 adults in 33 countries on six continents were surveyed. Buss found that females universally put more importance on resource-related characteristics in a partner, such as ambition, high intelligence and good financial prospects. Males, however, preferred younger mates and put more value on signs of a female's ability to reproduce, such as attractiveness and modesty. It is important to note that researchers were aware that the samples gathered cannot be representative of specific populations in all countries; however, the sample was relatively big.

  • On the contrary to biological approach, there are also social explanations of human relationships. One of them is familiarity and proximity.

  • **Zayonc (1968):** Familiarity influences liking as we trust and tend to like what we know. This phenomenon was investigated and as a result he proposed 'The mere exposure effect' which focuses on being repeatedly exposed to an object (person) is what eventually produces preference for that object (person).

  • Proximity also affects interpersonal relationships – being physically close with others increases the chances of meeting each other in the future.

  • **Festinger et al. (1950):** Closeness was examined by investigating the pattern of how people made friends as part of a new housing investment. Researchers discovered that proximity was key to establishing friendship. For example, people made friends with other people they met while performing their usual duties, such as throwing away garbage. 41% of people who lived close to each other claimed to be friends. So friendly relationships are established as a result of everyday spontaneous situations (e.g. when you run into each other by chance you must eventually engage in interaction, so eventually you need to create a positive relationship).

11. • **Conflict happens** if intergroup behaviour that benefits the interests of one group/person at the cost of another person/group escalates and becomes explicit; the conflict resolution focuses on conflict reduction using specific strategies.

  • **Muzafer Sherif (1954):** This studied the realistic theory of conflict: to find out what factors cause two groups to develop hostile relationships, and then see how to reduce this hostility. In particular, to see if two groups of boys can be manipulated into conflict through competition and then resolved through conflict. The participants were 12-year-old boys selected by lottery. They were divided into two equal groups. The boys called themselves 'Rattlers' and 'Eagles'. They arrived by separate buses and settled in their cabins in two places. They didn't know about the second group, thinking they were alone in the park. Each group had junior camp advisors (students earning money in the summer) who lived with the boys and oversaw their activities, and senior camp advisors were participating observers who stayed with boys for 12 hours a day. Sherif found that the boys did not need encouragement to be competitive. As soon as they learned about another group in the park, they resorted to the language 'us' and 'they' and wanted a baseball game – so the boys themselves began the friction phase. Sherif believes this study confirms his hypothesis about intergroup behaviour, especially realistic conflict theory.
    – Groups were created quickly, with hierarchies and leaders, without any encouragement from adults.
    – When groups meet in competitive situations, solidarity within the group increases, as does group hostility.
    – Friction is reduced when both groups are forced to cooperate, negotiate and share. Sherif calls this action toward overarching goals.
    – **Criticism**: The Sherif study is of high ecological validity. 22 boys were in a real summer camp (Robber Cave in Oklahoma) and had no idea that something unusual was happening. Actions such as pulling a truck seemed real to them. Sherif's study is also important because he used various methods such as watching and recording boys. He collected quantitative and qualitative data on their behaviour. For example, he gained friendship with the group at the end of the friction and integration phase, and found that how many Eagles the Rattlers boys chose as friends increased from 6.4% to 36.4%. Generalization would be difficult because the sample was biased (pre-teen boys from one culture). There may be possible signs of mental harm and fraud, as hostility was reported. The dependent variable would also be difficult to measure; moreover, demand characteristics could appear.

  • **Howarth (2002):** The aim of this study was to investigate how the struggle for recognition permeates everyday experiences in the context of young people living in Brixton, UK. Results were that people from Brixton thought it was a 'diverse, creative and vibrant' community; however, others had negative representations of being from Brixton. This influenced the identity of those in Brixton.

  • **Strengths and limitations of the study**: Triangulation, interviews and focus groups were used in this study, making it valid and reliable. It can also be easily replicated in different contexts and surrounding. The study was ethical; however, not entirely generalizable due to the sample used in the study.

12. • Prosocial behaviour's intention is to benefit other individuals or a group of people. We can be prosocial by volunteering, helping others, sharing sources or cooperating. **Altruism** is a form of prosocial behaviour – it is selfless helping (you don't get any benefit from it) and might even involve making a sacrifice for the sake of another person.

  • There is no one good way to explain altruism. Some explanations are based on biological basis (genetics and evolutionary arguments); however, other arguments are more cognitive (psychological altruism).

  • **Kin selection theory** is based on evolutionary theory. Its assumption is that we want our genes to survive, so the closer relatives are more likely to targeted by altruistic helping, as we share a significant amount of genes with them. An important aspect is that younger and healthy kin will be more likely to be helped because they are more likely to have children and pass genes on to the next generation.

  • **Madsen et al. (2007):** This study performed an experiment about kin selection with UK and South African students (16–45 years (reproductive age)). Participants were asked to perform a physical exercise that becomes increasingly painful: wall sits. Prior to the exercise, participants gave a list of biological relatives, including relatives that the participants lived with. UK participants were told prior to the wall sit that one biological relative would be randomly selected from the list and would receive payment according to the length that the participant could stay in the wall sit position. South African participants had the same exercise but their relatives were given food instead of payment. The UK students were the first into the experiment; then the South African students were asked to participate. Participants were allowed to stop at any time. The results were that the amount of time spent in the painful position increased with relatedness – people were more often ready to stay in this position for themselves than their parents, analogically more for parents in comparison to grandparents. The conclusion was that kinship is a significant factor which influences the probability of altruistic behaviour.

- Researchers used two different cultures to test their theory, so they took cross-cultural differences under consideration; however, the sample was biased in terms of gender (no women in the study). Also, due to the physical nature of the study some people could have problems performing the exercise regardless the reward.

- **Empathy altruism model:** This theory proposed by Batson claims that people tend to help others because they are concerned about their own wellbeing. So if one feels empathy towards another human being he/she will help even if there is a need to sacrifice. We experience two types of emotions when we see someone suffering: personal distress (this leads to egoistic helping) or empathetic concern (this one leads to altruistic helping).

- **Batson (1981):** To illustrate his theory, Batson performed a study called the **Elaine study**. The aim was to investigate the problem of making an empirical distinction between egoistic and altruistic motivation for helping. The behaviour (helping) can be directly observed. The challenge was to somehow use the behaviour as a basis for inferring whether the motivation underlying it was egoistic or altruistic. Researchers used 44 female psychology students. Participants were tested individually and filled out a questionnaire beforehand. They were led to believe that they were an observer of a girl, Elaine, who was being tested on digit recall. The description was given as relatable (high empathy) or unrelatable (low empathy). The participants watched a pre-recorded video of Elaine; after two trials she received electric shock and was finding the shocks unpleasant. Participants were asked if they would like to help her by taking her place. One half were told they could fill out a questionnaire and leave (easy escape condition). The other half were told they must watch the remaining eight trials before leaving (difficult escape condition). Participants in the low-empathy/easy-escape condition agreed to help only in 18% cases, so low empathy affected the motivation to help and made it more egoistic. High-empathy/easy-escape condition didn't have an effect on the probability of helping: more participants agreed to help in the easy-escape condition. Based on the results of the study and the fact that the motivation to help in the high-empathy condition was altruistic (not egoistic), we can accept empathy altruism theory and explain that genuine altruistic reactions are caused by empathetic concern.

- **Criticism:** The study was an experiment, so low-ecological validity is an issue. Participants were psychology female students so there is a clear sample bias (gender and psychology as a subject). There also could have been some issues with demand characteristics and behaving according to the presumable aim.

- Empathy altruism theory is contradictory towards evolutionary explanations of altruistic behaviour. The reason is that this assumption doesn't assume that altruism can be the result of selfish motivation. Kin selection theory doesn't explain spontaneous altruistic acts towards strangers. Unfortunately, much of the research about altruism is anecdotal in nature as we hear about sacrifice on TV news or from witnesses. These sources have no scientific quality.

Set A: Paper 3 (HL)

1a. • Overt naturalistic observation.
- One characteristic of this research method is that participants know they are being observed by the researcher.
- Another factor is that this type of observation is conducted in naturalistic settings – in this case, families were observed in their own homes.

1b. • Purposive sampling was used in this study.
- This sampling method focuses on finding people with specific traits: in this study, researchers were looking for families with one child of a specific age and gender.

- If the sampling is too limited, it may make it difficult to generalize results from the sample to a universal population.

1c. • **Semi structured interviews**: conversation-like interviews which would enable the researcher to get information directly from the parents regarding their attitude towards their toddler children. It could be more effective than the current method, as there is the risk that people react to being observed. In other words, there currently may be reactivity involved (behaviour can be changed due to the fact that they are taking part in the study).

2. • Participants were informed of the observation being conducted (informed consent was provided).
- It is possible that because of demand characteristics, there may be more or fewer behaviours than the parents would normally criticize when they are not being observed. This potentially can result in psychological harm (children could receive more negative reactions from their parents).
- Mild deception was used, as the participants were not told that the study will focus on the gender of children.
- The children should remain anonymous.
- Parents who don't want their children to participate have a right to withdraw from the study at any time.
- Although this is a naturalistic observation, parents should still be debriefed on the findings of the study.

3. Types of generalization in qualitative research:
- Representational generalization – the results of the study can be applied to a wider population.
- Inferential generalization (transferability) – the results of the study can be applied to other groups of people or different external settings.

Potential issues with generalization in this study:
- Only one culture was taken under consideration (USA).
- Small sample size (24 families).
- Sampling bias (white, middle-class, university-background families).
- Purposive sampling itself could have an effect on possible generalization, as a specific group of people is being targeted.

Set B: Paper 1 (SL and HL): Section A

1. • Pheromones are chemicals released into the environment by a member of one species and received by another individual of the same species. These substances have no smell, and their role in humans remains uncertain since adults have no functioning vomeronasal organ, which processes pheromone signals in animals. Most of pheromones are responsible for sexual behaviour and attractiveness.

- **Wedekind et al. (1995):** This study was on the effects of pheromones on adults. 44 male students were asked to wear the same T-shirt for two nights in a row. The T-shirt was kept in a plastic bag during the day. Men were asked to keep the smell as neutral as possible by avoiding sexual activity, smoking, eating spicy food or using perfumed products and products that produced a strong smell. After two nights, 49 female students were asked to rate six T-shirts for pleasure and fragrance intensity. Prior to the study, all male and female participants were classified for similarity to the immune systems (Major Histocompatibility Complex). Researchers discovered that women consistently preferred the smell of men whose immune system differs from their own (MHC dissimilar men), but only when they do not use birth control pills. The reason of this could be the fact that the more dissimilar the immune system, the better chances of survival of future offspring. These results suggest that sweat contains pheromones or pheromones that may affect mate preferences.

2. • Thinking and decision-making may seem like a straightforward and trustworthy process. However, it holds many cognitive biases that mislead our beliefs on topics and lead to issues such as stereotypes and generalizations of particular social groups. One cognitive bias is an illusory correlation, which refers to the belief that two factors are related/associated when there is no or only a minor association.

- **Hamilton & Rose (1980):** This studied how illusory correlations maintain social stereotypes of particular groups or occupations. They conducted three experiments with undergraduate students and adult participants: 77 females and 73 males. In the first experiment, the volunteers were made to read adjectives and traits that described someone of a particular occupancy, with the inclusion of some non-stereotypical adjectives. The second experiment included adjectives that were either consistent or unrelated to the stereotypes of the occupational groups. In the third study, traits were inconsistent with the stereotypes of the groups. Participants were asked to estimate how often each of the traits described members of certain jobs or positions.

- The study showed a sign of systematic biases in the responses, as the participants showed correlation with congruency between the adjectives and the jobs in terms of their stereotypes instead of the actual causes. Noticeably, the participants ordered the new information by the stereotypical belief. Due to this, the researchers found that correlations and cognitive biases as such come from two rare events occur simultaneously. Humans assume that this must relate in all cases.

3. • A sociocultural approach to behaviour investigates individuals and their behaviour in groups. Many studies were done to investigate the influence of the group on a single human being. One potential ethical issue in empirical research in this area is psychological harm, especially when it comes to studies done on children.

- **Bandura, Ross & Ross (1961):** The aim of this study was to investigate to what extent the aggressive behaviour of adult role models affects children's behaviour, meaning that the children would then imitate this aggressive behaviour. 72 children (36 males/36 females) of about four years old took part in this study. Children were rated on their level of aggression beforehand. Children then observed adults behaving in aggressive/non-aggressive ways towards a Bobo doll (such as punching, kicking, pushing or throwing). Afterwards, the children were taken to the room with aggressive/nonaggressive toys (including a Bobo doll) and left to play while being observed by researchers. Children were showed more aggressive behaviour towards the Bobo doll after observing an aggressive model. They also imitated same-sex model more often. The study shows that aggression can be learned through observational learning.

- One important ethical consideration in this study is psychological harm, which means causing undue stress to participants. Children could experience long-lasting effects of this study by showing aggressive behaviour not only to Bobo doll but also towards other children or their parents. This in turn may have a serious negative effect on the children and their environment in future years. As a result, exposing children to adult violence against the Bobo was a significant ethical consideration.

Set B: Paper 1 (SL and HL): Section B

4. • Evolution is a process of changes that occurs over time due to changes in heritable traits that are passed from generation to generation. Evolutionary explanations in psychology can be applied to explain human behaviour. One of them is disgust, the emotion responsible for avoidance of pathogens, which serves as the first line of defence against infections.

- **Curtis, Aunger, Rabie (2004):** This study conducted a correlational study using a survey placed on a BBC website. Its aim was to test several predictions about disgust: disgust must be stronger in response to stimuli associated with disease, there will be a cross-cultural similarity in disgust responses, females will have a stronger disgust response as they have to protect the immune system of their babies, and disgust response should be weaker with age. The sample size was about 77,000 volunteers from 165 countries. Participants were asked to rate 20 pictures for disgust from 1 to 5. Each pair presented disease salient fluid and the other chemically looking fluid in various forms. All predictions were confirmed. Women rated disease-salient pictures as more disgusting than men; organic-looking fluid was rated as more disgusting in general; answers correlated with previously predicted age (older people rated it less disgusting); results were also consistent cross-culturally. Results of the study supported the evolutionary explanation that disgust evolved from protection from disease and can be explained through theory of evolution. This suggests that disgust is a biologically based response to dangerous stimuli that reduces the risk of infectious disease.

- **Fessler (2005):** The study investigated whether the emotion of disgust plays a role in infectious disease protection. This hypothesis was tested by measuring the level of disgust in a group of pregnant women in various trimesters. A web survey was completed by 496 women in different trimesters (1st, 2nd and 3rd) and the average age of participants was 28. Women in the first trimester reported higher levels of disgust compared to women in other trimesters. They also reported more nausea.

The results of this study supports the hypothesis that disgust sensitivity varies when it comes to pregnancy and serves as the protection from dangerous, infectious diseases.

- Both studies seem to confirm evolutionary explanation of disgust. Both studies used online surveys to gather data; this is not the most reliable source of information as it is very subjective self-reported responses (meaning there is no possibility to judge the extent that responses were honest or if the 'screw you' effect could bias results). Studies also may cause researchers to be susceptible to confirmation bias, meaning they see what they expect to see.

- Evolutionary explanations of behaviour are very difficult to test. This is a phenomenon that needs a possible explanation, and so there is a risk that because we need justification we find one. However, not all evolutionary explanations are valid cross-culturally, so specific phenomena that are thought to be universal can be explained by using different (e.g. sociocultural) arguments; The best-fit approach would work with the eclectic approach to explain various behaviours, as this allows different factors to be taken under consideration. Evolutionary theories also lack knowledge about prehistoric environments; therefore, many explanations and comparisons between presence and past are hypothetical and as a result could be flawed. Many conclusions are made based on animal behaviour. Although there are physiological and genetic similarities between humans and animals, it is impossible to draw conclusions based on different species. As both studies show evolutionary arguments but do not establish cause and effect, they are mainly descriptive and not explanatory.

5. **(SL option)**
- **Schemas** – or mental representations of knowledge – are based on previous experiences and human memory. Different types of schemas (for example, self-schemas, scripts and social schemas) help us to make sense of the world around us. We learn what behavior is or isn't appropriate. Schemas could also be changed throughout our life. *Self-schemas* refer to us (what we know about ourselves like our strengths/weaknesses); *scripts* are about situations or skills (what to do and how to do it); *social schemas* more generally refer to groups of people and how we perceive them (such as stereotypes).

- Humans are information processors, this is why we actively gain and recall information (by encoding and retrieval), we tend to implement existing knowledge into new information. Jean Piaget (the author of the Theory of Cognitive Development) explained assimilation and accommodation in terms of how schemas are created: assimilation happens when new information needs to be changed (adjusted) to fit an existing schema and accommodation is when the existing schema is not accurate and needs to be modified because of the existence of some new information.

- **Frederic Bartlett (1932)** investigated schemas in his study entitled 'The War of the Ghosts'. Bartlett aimed to determine how social and cultural factors influence schemas and hence can lead to memory distortions.
  - Participants used were from an English background.
  - They were asked to read 'The War of the Ghosts' – a Native American folk tale.
  - Their memory was tested of the story using serial reproduction and repeated reproduction, where they were asked to recall it six or seven times over various retention intervals.
  - Serial reproduction: the first participant reading the story reproduces it on paper, which is then read by a second participant who reproduces the first participant's reproduction, and so on until it is reproduced by six or seven different participants.
  - Repeated reproduction: the same participant reproduces the story six or seven times from their own previous reproductions. Their reproductions occur between time intervals from 15 minutes to as long as several years.

As the number of reproductions increased, the story became shorter and there were more changes to the story. For example, 'hunting seals' changed into 'fishing' and 'canoes' became 'boats'.

These changes show the alteration of culturally unfamiliar things into what the English participants were culturally familiar with.

This makes the story more understandable according to the participants' experiences and cultural background (schemas).

Results indicated that recalled stories were distorted and altered in various ways making it more conventional and acceptable to their own cultural perspective (rationalization).

The study has low temporal validity, there is also an issue with a cause and effect relationships as IV have not been manipulated and there was no control group; the study was done on UK participants only; instructions given to participants were unclear and not standardized.

- Memory is a reconstructive process and it is based on pre-existing schemas. Bartlett's study helped to explain through the understanding of schemas when people remember stories, they typically omit ('leave out') some details, and introduce rationalizations and distortions, because they reconstruct the story so as to make more sense in terms of their knowledge, the culture in which they were brought up in and experiences in the form of schemas. Bartlett's study shows how schema theory is useful for understanding how people categorize information, interpret stories, and make inferences. It also contributes to the understanding of cognitive distortions in memory. It also showed the relationship between schemas and encoding as well as the retrieval of memories; familiar schemas help us to integrate new information into an existing one.

- **Loftus & Palmer (1974)** – The aim of the study was to investigate how post-event information (schemas in the form of leading questions) affects the memory of a witness. The participants were shown a short clip (30s) of a car crash. Afterwards, they were asked to provide answers for the questionnaire. The question was "About how fast were the cars going when they 'smashed', 'collided', 'bumped', 'contacted', 'hit' each other?". Each group was given a different word, chosen from the ones listed above. Outcomes presented that the estimated speed when the words 'smashed' and 'collided' occurred was significantly higher (40.8 and 39.3 mph) than in case of the words with lighter association. The researchers concluded that the intensity of the word used and the attitude towards it (schemas) affects the height of the speed suggested by participants. The word smash and its intensity seems to be related to pre-existing knowledge and experience. Whereas the word collided doesn't fit in with this kind of schema and is perceived not to be as intense. As the information was provided, the memory processes of retrieval started to bring out the pre-existing memories associated with the word. The verb used fit in with that schema.

- The study effectively isolated IV by classifying groups into different verbs; the cause and effect was established; the study lacks ecological validity as it was a lab experiment, however confounding variables were controlled. Students participated in the study – this is not a representative sample, as they could have been biased.

- Schema theory helps to predict behavior as it refers to many common situations; many different studies across different cultures have been done to illustrate how schema theory works; its usefulness refers specifically to other cognitive processes – it helps to understand the active and reconstructive nature of memory.

5. **(HL option)**
- Digital technology affects a wide array of cognitive processes. The constant availability and use of digital devices means that individuals' cognitive processes have adapted to these technologies. Phenomena such as cognitive offloading (the outsourcing of cognitive work to technology) or enhancement of visual working memory results from continuous play of action video games.

- Laboratory research claims **(Ophir et al. 2009)** reported that multitasking impairs performance and that the brain cannot not perform tasks simultaneously, and just switches from task to task quickly. Each time we change tasks, there is a stop-start process that goes on in our brains and it is far from efficient as we make more mistakes and it takes more time, concentration and energy. Since there is an increase in availability and dependency of digital technology, students tend to 'media-multitask' by either texting during classes or having a quick scroll through Facebook.

- A study by **Wood et al. (2011)** conducted a laboratory experiment that aimed to compare retention of information in a simulated class environment between participants simultaneously using digital media services (e.g. Facebook, MSN) and those with access only to physical writing tools. The study involved an opportunity sample of university students. After being given a lecture, participants completed a multiple-choice test on the information presented to them. Consistently, those who did not have access to digital technologies outperformed those who did. This would indicate that the presence of digital technologies in many classroom settings is likely to exacerbate distraction and 'multitasking' practices that are detrimental to learning. Researchers contextualized these findings through the concept of a cognitive bottleneck, in which the need for a common cognitive resource (attention) decreases the efficiency of multiple activities (e.g. to write a note or send a message) that simultaneously need that resource. However, these findings applied primarily to more engaging media, such as Facebook. Less visually engaging media, such as MSN, caused lesser discrepancies in test scores, indicating that the degree of distraction may depend on the nature of technology one is using to 'multitask'. However, the simulated nature of the lecture meant that participants lacked a direct incentive to focus (while real classes have grades, punishments, etc.) reducing the ecological validity of the study.

- The effects of multitasking with digital technology while learning may affect different kinds of memory in different ways. A field experiment by **Glass and Kang (2017)** aimed to establish how detrimental the use of technology during lectures would be in a real-world scenario. Participants were a purposive sample of university students who were placed in one of two groups; all were taking the same university course: One group was allowed to use technology during their lectures, while the other group was not. Student performance (memory) was measured in quiz questions during lectures, as well as unit and final exams. All participants performed similarly during in-class quizzes, regardless of access to technology; however, participants with access to technology performed more poorly in exams. These findings suggest that access to digital technology does not impair the ability to remember something in the short-term, but does affect long-term retention. Researchers suggest this is because while in class participants could redirect their attention from a digital distraction to the information necessary to answer a question; however, behaviours such as note taking and direct attention to a lecture do not receive priority when using technology is an option for participants, making their memories less strong and long-lasting. These results have a high degree of ecological validity, as the experiment took place in a real classroom scenario in which students were incentivized by their grades to perform well both on the quizzes and exams involved.

- Despite multiple studies demonstrating how multitasking with technology can negatively affect memory, a laboratory experiment by **Rosen et al. (2011)** aimed to look more specifically at what student behaviours can have moderating effects regarding memory of lectures. Three different groups in an opportunity sample of university students received a varying amount of texts (low, moderate, high) during a videotaped lecture. While those who received more texts performed more poorly than those who received fewer, these results represented a total discrepancy of only ~10% between the high and low text volume groups. More importantly, there were other factors correlated with quiz performance that had more significant effects: the study also measured the number of words written by participants in all their texts, as well as how long it took them to respond to texts. Participants who waited for longer periods of time before sending responses performed better on quizzes, as well as students who sent a smaller number of words across their texts. These results indicate that while multitasking between lectures and texts or other digital stimuli may negatively impact memory, behavioural measures can mitigate these effects. Namely, results indicate that choosing opportune moments to switch to texting (e.g. when there is lecture content of minimal importance) and minimizing time spent distracted overall (in this case by typing fewer words) are effective strategies for minimizing the detrimental effects of multitasking. Because the lecture was related to the content of the participants' university course, there was a degree of ecological validity.

- As seen in the above studies, media multitasking has a detrimental impact on the cognitive process of memory. The studies above have followed the ethical requirements of psychological research through informed consent, debriefing, right of withdrawal, protection from harm and confidentiality. They were all empirical studies that employed observation in a natural setting and that created ecological validity; however, in the first two studies; the texts were between research assistants, which made them less ecologically valid. The samples of the studies had significantly more females than males, which could affect the generalizability of the research. One must also consider the possibility of researcher bias, participant bias and

social desirability bias when considering the studies. Overall the studies provide a good framework into research on how digital technology can affect the cognitive process of memory.
- There is significant research that suggests that multitasking with digital technology while learning does decrease memory of content. However, these effects seem to vary depending on the nature of the technology, a person's behaviour, and how memory is tested. Technology seems to impair long-term retention more than short-term memorization, for example. In addition, flashier, more distracting technology causes more pronounced deficiencies in memory. However, if individuals minimize the volume of time spent using technology (multi-tasking), choose opportune moments to do so, and are motivated to perform, these effects can be mitigated to an extent.

6. (SL option)
- A dimension represents the preference to one type of behaviour in a given culture. One cultural dimension is individualism vs collectivism, which is the extent to which a culture values individuals taking care of themselves and not demonstrating dependency on others (individualism) or seeing individuals as members of social groups that take care of each other in exchange for loyalty (collectivism). These different values are learned through a process of socialization (the internalization of cultural norms).
- **Berry (1967)** is a lab experiment with the aim of investigating how dimension I-C influenced the behavior of conformity. The sample consisted of Tenme people of Sierra Leone (who are part of a collectivist culture) and Inuit people of Canada (who are part of individualist society). It recreated the Asch's (1955) paradigm experiment. Each individual was brought into a room by him or herself. For the test, they were given a set of nine lines. They were asked to match the line that most closely matched another line. Each of the participants stated their opinion aloud. The researchers found that the majority of Tenme people demonstrated conformity in their answer to match the rest of the group. Conversely, they found that only a small part of the Inuit people conformed their answer to the rest of the group. The researchers thus concluded that since the Tenme culture was collectivist with agricultural economy and valued cooperation, the conformity behavior will be a common phenomenon. They also concluded that since Inuit culture is individualistic and emphasizes self-sufficiency in practices such as child rearing, conformity is not a common behavior. Thus, this study illustrates the role of cultural dimension in human behavior.
- **Petrova et al. (2007)** prepared the study to investigate if I-C dimension affects the level of compliance between cultures. She focused on Foot in the door technique. 3000 Asian and US students sample were asked to take part in the short voluntary online survey about relationships. 1 month after the survey participants received another request to take part in another survey which would take more time than the previous one (40 mins instead of 20 mins). Compliance with the initial request had a stronger impact on subsequent compliance among the U.S. participants than among the Asian participants. The findings of stronger consistency with past choices in individualistic cultures than in collectivistic cultures suggest that the stronger the cultural orientation toward individualism, the stronger the effect is of past personal commitments on future compliance. That is, once participants have chosen to comply with a request, individualists should be more likely than collectivists to comply with subsequent, similar requests. This study shows that I-C cultural dimension affects human behavior in terms of the level of compliance.
- Evaluation of research:
  - Many of studies are artificial in nature so it's not possible to generalize them to natural settings.
  - Possible ecological validity issues.
  - There is the question in terms of how the researcher's attitude and their own biases affect the whole procedure of the study and the results.
  - Studies done in laboratory settings – on one hand cause and effect could be established, confounding variables could be controlled.
  - Surveys used as RMs are quick and convenient ways to gather data however subjective, the answers are based on self-assessment.
  - Some studies were done many years ago, so the temporal validity is questionable.
  - Cultural dimensions could be too vague to operationalize.

- Some results of studies which investigate specific cultures (e.g. Petrova) should also consider different factors possibly having an effect on behavior (e.g. acculturation); moreover, the use of English language could potentially affect the results of this study.

6. (HL option)
- **Globalization** is the ongoing process in which the world is becoming more interconnected and interdependent in the areas of trade in both goods and services; many elements of culture; communication; and transport. The exponential increase in the use of technology can be seen as the catalyst for the more intense worldwide connections within the world currently. Psychological influence of globalisation is mainly focused on how people from different cultures make sense of different aspects of this phenomenon.
- Immigration is a huge part of globalisation and may cause the process of enculturation (local influences) and acculturation (global influences) to be forced to merge even if they're not compatible. Ethnic groups/nations all undergo three processes within social identity theory: categorisation, social identification and social comparison, resulting in giving each group a sense of identity and belonging.
- A negative impact of globalization is that first-generation immigrants often feel that their personal culture isn't well-suited to their local culture and can cause symptoms of depression and anxiety. The study **Gonzales et al. (2004)** aimed to investigate whether or not migration stressors, such as choice of migration and discrimination, are associated with the psychological well-being of young first-generation Latino immigrants. A stratified cluster sample design of 280 Latino immigrant teenagers living in the USA was used to collect survey data. The anxiety and depression symptom levels of the Latino youth and the overall youth of America were measured, and symptoms were more prevalent in the Latino community. This suggested that immigration, a significant aspect of globalization, causes the Latino youth to have a negative view of global cultural influences interfering with their formerly local cultural influences.
- **Criticism**: This study may not be the most credible for this argument because it also suggests that migration may not be the only cause for those depressive symptoms. It provides evidence for the fact that support from home and school affect the chance of a child having depressive symptoms, thus proving to an extent that migration stressors are not the only cause. Additionally, this study supports evidence for the fact that globalization through the means of immigration is also positive. The survey results suggest that the immigrants who received a positive and welcoming reaction received a lot less acculturative stress, giving them a sense of social belonging and a positive attitude towards their identity. This means their psychological well-being was unharmed/less harmed by migration stressors and they may even be motivated to pursue opportunities they wouldn't have had in their countries of origin. However, this study had a relatively small sample size that was only aimed at teenagers, which is a small part of the Latino community in the US and therefore an even smaller sample in relation to all immigrants. This makes the sample fairly unrepresentative. Also, discrimination comes in a multitude of forms so it's difficult to measure. Additionally, the methodology of surveying is quite restrictive because the participants may have not understood the importance of giving accurate answers.
- **Biculturalism** is another product of globalization through the form of immigration, in which people who have a moderate–high association with more than one culture may self-identify as bicultural. Culture is made up of schemas, so bicultural people have access to more than one schema and use the most applicable one in everyday situations.
- **Chen et al. (2008)** aimed to investigate how bicultural identity integration (BII) is related to psychological adjustment and well-being. Questionnaires were used to assess cultural identity and well-being within three groups of participants: mainland Chinese immigrants, Filipino sojourners and bilingual college students in Hong Kong and China. The sample was gathered through volunteer and opportunity sampling and these groups were chosen because they all differ in acculturation pressures and status. The questionnaire data was used to create a score for psychological adjustment and the results suggest that the people with a higher BII score also have a higher psychological adjustment score. This means that the integration of bicultural identities is important for positive psychological results. Overall, this suggests that globalisation has a positive influence that supplies people with a positive attitude towards biculturalism. This case is relevant

because it provides single cultural context and it's a fairly recent study too. However, there are limits too, such as the fact that it's a correlational study and so doesn't provide a reason for the correlation. Also, it's limited to Hong Kong and a longitudinal approach would've been more appropriate.

- On the other hand, it can be argued that biculturalism is only positive when the individuals can balance all elements of their cultures. Some less-fortunate people feel they don't belong to either cultures they've grown up with. **Lyons-Padilla et al. (2015)** used a survey aimed at Muslim immigrants living in the USA to investigate attitudes towards acculturation and biculturalism in first- and second-generation immigrants. They concluded that marginalisation can cause immigrants to rebel against the country they live in if they don't feel it has cultural relevance to them. This could be a reason for the increase in terrorism over the last 20 or so years because the intensity of globalization has also increased. Therefore, this study supports evidence for the negative impact globalization has on the world. This is credible because it's a very recent study and again provides single cultural context. However, a longitudinal study may have been better in order to make it more valid because culture is a dynamic concept and people's acceptance abilities are also ever-changing.

- In conclusion, globalization influences behaviour and attitudes towards biculturalism and acculturation in a plethora of ways that are both positive and negative. Social identity theory, marginalisation and migration stressors may provide reasoning for the ways in which globalisation influences these concepts.

Set B: Paper 2 (SL and HL)

1. • **Abnormal psychology** is an area of psychology which focuses on severe behavioural patterns that don't follow social norms (mental disorders). The aim of abnormal psychology is also to describe/explain/analyse/criticize abnormal behaviour.

- This can be done by using different approaches: abnormality as a deviation from social norms, which are generally acceptable; abnormality explained by different criteria proposed by **Rosenhan & Seligman (1984)**; abnormality understood as not fulfilling the requirements of mental health **(Jahoda, 1958)**; as a statistical model (abnormal behaviour is a behaviour which is statistically uncommon); or as a medical approach to abnormality (using mental classification systems to identify unique symptoms of every individual).

- **Diagnosis** of mental disorders is a way to classify patterns of abnormal behaviour based on their common characteristics or symptoms.

- **Medical model** focuses on symptoms to define abnormality. With a specific set of observed symptoms for every mental illness comes a set of causes and appropriate treatment. Classification systems (e.g. DSM-V, ICD 10, CCMD 3) are used to mainly described such symptoms and differentiate them from other symptoms and different disorders.

- When it comes to defining abnormality, one of the most commonly acquired approaches is the mental illness criterion, also known as the medical model. It is based on the assumption that abnormal behaviour has specific origins. This view is closely linked to psychiatry and entails that patients are seen as 'ill', just like those suffering from physiological illnesses. Clinicians try to identify and classify abnormal behaviour, using observations, patients' self-reports, clinical interviews and diagnostic manuals (such as DSM-V), which classify symptoms of specific disorders. This diagnosis aims to find suitable treatment for the patient and make a prognosis.

- This approach has its strengths: some may argue that it is an advantage to be called 'sick' because it suggests that people with mental disorders are not fully responsible for their state and actions. It also shows that mental illness can be as serious as a physiological one. On the other hand, being classified as 'ill' can be a disadvantage as in many cultures and societies there is still a stigma surrounding mental illness, and thus being diagnosed may negatively affect the way other people perceive us. Also, treating psychological disorders as somewhat equal to physiological illnesses may be faulty. Although the origin of some mental disorders can be linked to physiological changes in the brain, the majority can't. Szasz (one of the greatest critics of this approach) argues with the whole concept of 'mental illness' and suggests that psychological disorders should rather be seen as 'problems of living' and that they are in no way equal to 'real' physiological illnesses.

- One of the studies into the medical model is the study on being sane in insane places conducted by **Rosenhan (1973)**. The aim of this study was to test those two factors in a natural environment

and see if psychiatrists were able to diagnose people as 'sane' or 'insane'. Eight participants took part in the study, including Rosenhan. They were told to report hearing voices. All of the participants were admitted to different psychiatric hospitals in the USA. Each participant from then on acted normally, not presenting any other symptoms of mental disorders. All of them were admitted to the hospitals with diagnosed schizophrenia, with an exception of one participant diagnosed with manic depression. As patients, they took notes on their time being hospitalized; however, hospital staff interpreted this as a symptom of their illness. They were released after 7–52 days with a diagnosis of schizophrenia in remission. After publishing the study, Rosenhan got messages from psychiatric hospitals claiming that it would never happen in their institution, so a follow-up study was conducted. In this variation, Rosenhan contacted hospitals and told them that he would send pseudo-patients. Almost half of admitted patients were recognized as impostors by at least one psychiatrist or staff member, while no impostors were actually sent. The study raised awareness of invalid diagnoses and had an impact on perceiving psychiatry. It prompted a revision of diagnostic procedures and discussion about consequences of diagnoses.

- **Criticism:** The study is said to be unethical since it employed deception and possible consequences for the psychiatric hospitals; however, the results were so beneficial that it justified the procedure. The follow-up study could have caused issues as actual patients were 'recognized' as imposters which could have negatively affected the treatment they had received. It clearly shows that medical model of abnormality is not effective when it comes to the identification of symptoms. One can refer to **sick role bias,** which means that hearing about symptoms can result in doctors diagnosing the patient with reference to classification systems and their previous experience. However, this study is quite old and so will not be in line with modern practices. DSM II was used at that time, as there was a different understanding of abnormal behaviour 50 years ago.

- **Parker et al. (2001):** Researchers investigated two sets of depressed outpatients: Chinese living in Malaysia and Caucasian in Australia (50 participants in general). Patients were asked to rate the extent to which they experienced each of 39 symptoms in the last week. The questionnaire required them to complete an inventory of both somatic and cognitive symptoms, and rank the three items from the least to the most distressing. Results of the study showed that the Chinese were significantly more likely to identify a somatic symptom as their presenting complaint (60 % vs 13 %), while the Australian participants were more likely to identify depressed mood, cognitive and anxiety items. Responses clearly showed that the Chinese did score somewhat higher on a somatic set of items, but differed far more significantly in being less likely to affirm cognitive items of depression, resulting in lower total inventory scores. Variation across the contrast samples in acknowledging the presence of symptoms did not relate simply to the prevalence of those symptoms. Emotional and cognitive symptoms of depression (thinking, memory problems, low mood and helplessness) were more often identified by Australian participants than Chinese ones. The difference is evident. Western individual cultures perceive abnormal behaviours in different, less stigmatizing way, and discussing emotional wellbeing is quite common. This is unlike Eastern, collectivist cultures, where experiencing emotional problems and discussing them is the sign of weakness and can be stigmatizing.

- The study used questionnaires, which is a self-reported way to gather data. As a result, biased data can be provided by participants (subjectivity can be an issue). Memory is not a fully reliable cognitive process, so patients could be mistaken when they identify their symptoms (demand characteristics).

- In general, the medical model needs to be considered cross culturally to apply differences between cultures in terms of mental illness perception as well as methodology. All studies investigating abnormal behaviour should be done on various groups of people to avoid sample or gender biases. As Parker's study shows, some culturally bound behaviours can influence results of different studies. As the example of DSM shows, perception of mental illnesses has changed throughout the time (homosexuality was included in DSM II as mental illness) and much research made in the past followed outdated classification systems that wouldn't be seen as accurate today.

2. • **Prevalence** is the proportion of people from a specific population who suffer from the given disorder currently or in a given time interval.

- **Brown & Harris (1978):** This study investigated the link between depression and life events in 539 London women. They used interviews to ask women about specific life events which occurred in the past year. Then the researchers looked at these events and analysed them in comparison to depressive symptoms. There was a significant link between negative life events and the prevalence of depression. High levels of stress and negative past events made people more vulnerable to depression. 80% of women who suffered from major depressive disorder (MDD) had experienced a significant negative life situation in past year. The most important life events were lack of intimate relationship, lack of employment, and having three or more children at home. It's clearly visible that prevalence of MDD is strongly affected by external factors.
- **Criticism:** This was once one of the pioneering studies in this area; however, some criticism is needed here. Limitations could include sampling bias (only women were investigated, but the sample size was big enough to avoid possible generalization). Using interviews is a strength of the study as this is a reliable qualitative research method; however, self-reported information lowers the objectivity of provided data. As with any qualitative research (and unlike experiments) this type of research method doesn't allow researchers to identify cause-and-effect relationships, so the results are mainly correlational. This means bidirectional ambiguity could play a role and it is also possible that different factors (biological and/or cognitive) could be significant.
- **Nolen-Hoeksema (2000):** The aim of this study was to investigate the role of rumination in symptoms associated with depression. 1,132 participants from San Francisco took part in the study. Researchers interviewed participants twice a year. Among others, Beck Depression Inventory was used. The questionnaire asked participants to rate how often they experienced negative thoughts of a specific kind. Participants who showed symptoms of MDD at the time of the first interview had a significantly higher result in ruminant responses than participants who did not show any signs of MDD. Participants who were never depressed had significantly lower rumination results than other participants. This study clearly contributes to our understanding of prevalence rates of psychological disorder such as depression. The prevalence rate of MDD is much higher in women and rumination is a significant factor in this diagnosis.
- **Criticism:** The study is based on self-reported data again, so participants were not formally diagnosed with depression, meaning some information provided by participants could be flawed. Around 1,300 participants took part in the study so this is a relatively big number; however, it is not enough for generalization. This study seems to confirm Beck's theory of MDD.
- The following should be taken under consideration: People start experiencing symptoms at different ages. In many cases prevalence rates are based on official hospital records. There could be an issue of overpathologization and underpathologization of specific social groups. Researcher bias (and sick role bias) can affect the prevalence rates. Classification systems are not ideal so it is difficult to distinguish between true prevalence and some estimations made by different clinicians. There are significant differences in prevalence rates across cultures, meaning members of different societies may express their symptoms in more psychological or physiological ways, which can potentially result in biased diagnosis.

3.
- Treatment of disorders (e.g. depression) can be done by using biological and psychological therapies. Both have different assumptions and effects. Psychotherapy (mostly cognitive behavioural therapy (CBT)) is focused on Beck's cognitive theory of depression and deals with cognitive errors (automatic thinking which leads to some irrational behavioural patterns). Biological treatment is focused on chemicals in the brain as the main reason of this disorder. To fight this cause, patients should use medications (e.g. antidepressants) to restore the balance of neurotransmitters.
- Two research methods discussed in this response are: experiment and interview.
- **Jacobson et al. (1996):** The aim of this experiment was to check the effectiveness of CBT in treatment of depression. The comparison included the random assignment of 150 outpatients suffering from major depressive disorder (MDD) to three conditions: full CBT treatments, treatment involving both behavioural activation and teaching skills to modify automatic thoughts, and behavioural activation only. Self-reports were used, as well as observation of potential behavioural changes

in patients' behaviour. The results showed that there was no evidence that full treatment gave better results, both after acute treatment and after 6 months of follow-up, than both components. Behavioural activation and automatic thoughts treatment were as effective as CBT in changing negative thinking as well as dysfunctional attribution styles.
  - The research method used in this study was an experiment with the use of different ways to gather data (questionnaires and semi-structured interviews). This study is difficult when it comes to conclusions as there is probability of not direct cause-and-effect relationship. Some non-specific factors could have played a role in the assessment of effectiveness of treatment methods. Most of the experiment's strengths are based on the direct control of conditions and variables during the procedure. This experiment was conducted by using three conditions with one independent variable and one dependent variable, and participants were randomly allocated to conditions. The dependent variable was difficult to be operationalized as the effectiveness of therapy is subjective and hard to be measured. There are also some additional factors, such as the behaviour of therapists (which can potentially affect the results of the study due to participants being more motivated because of a researcher's personality). What is more, the researcher's expectations consciously or unconsciously could have affected the results of the study. This can be dealt with by using double blind control (when participants and researchers don't know which group is experimental or control).
- **Naeem et al. (2012):** The aim of this study was to construct a culturally specific cognitive behavioural therapy programme as well as assess its effectiveness. Nine depressed participants took part in the study. During the interviews they were asked about the treatment and their opinions about the illness itself. Some additional information was provided from a professional practice of one of the clinicians. All of the data was analysed using inductive content analysis. Basing on interpretations, researchers identified four main areas of investigation: participants' perception of an illness, reasons of depression, reference for help and their experience of treatment of depression. The result of this study was the possibility to develop a culturally specific version of CBT with translation and the use of local language terms.
  - The main research method used in this study was an interview, which is a qualitative research method. This was chosen because the study was performed in a new environment (Pakistan) and researchers didn't know much about the society. Another reason was the aim of the study: researchers were aiming to come up with a new tailored version of culturally specific CBT, so they needed opinions, perceptions, views and individual histories of participants. A quantitative research method (e.g. experiment) wouldn't allow them to get this type of information (more numerical results in experiment). However, when using inductive content analysis (ICA) there are both strengths and limitations: on one hand there is no previous assumption (hypothesis) which a researcher would want to refute or accept (researcher bias is eliminated); on the other hand, ICA is a very subjective process which is based on researcher's interpretations of information provided by participants. Also, being an interviewee can result in different behaviour and reactivity.
- Overall both types of research methods are accurate when it comes to treatment investigation. However, these methods should be used cautiously not to result in the research method determining the results of the study. This could make the application of results irrelevant.

4.
- Development as a learner is strongly connected with brain functioning (neuroplasticity, localization of function and neurotransmission). At a young age, neurogenesis and the relationship between the function and brain structure are very significant. Brain-imaging technology is used to provide information about the brain development and some brain processes while participants are involved in some activities.
- **Rosenzweig and Bennet (1972):** The study aimed to demonstrate the effect of enriched or deprived environment on neuroplasticity and as a result can be used in the context of brain development in developing as a learner. Their study is an example of animal studies, because they use rats placed in different environments. It was a lab experiment establishing a cause-and-effect relationship between the enrichment (the independent variable), where the deprived environment had no toys and the enriched had toys, and the change of mass of the rats' brains (dependent variable).

After 1–2 months the rats were euthanized and researchers found that animals from stimulating environment had heavier brains, including the frontal lobe (which is connected with the processes of thinking and decision-making). The results may suggest the impact of the stimulating environment on developing the brain cortex and creating new connections. A strength of this study is having the variables strictly under control. It highlights the importance of education in the growth of new synapses; however, it is questionable if a study made on rats can be generalized to humans. It is also undefined what an enriched environment means for a specific person. The question of ethical treatment of animals is also noteworthy.

- **Luby (2012):** The aim of the study was to measure the role of parental nurturing on the development of the hippocampus (this brain structure is responsible for passing on information from STM to LTM). In a long-term study of 92 depressive and healthy preschool children who had undergone neuroimaging (MRI) at school age, researchers checked whether early maternal support predicted volume of the hippocampus. The mother's support (nurturing) observed in early childhood strongly predicted hippocampus volume (10% larger than non-nurturing mothers) measured at school age (after 4 years). The positive effect of mother support on hippocampus volume was greater in children without depression. These findings provide prospective evidence in humans for the positive effects of early supportive parenting on the healthy development of the hippocampus, a key brain region for memory and stress modulation.

- The RM used in this study was natural experiment with no chance to control all variables as they were happening spontaneously. What is very important is the term **nurturing** – it's very broad (including emotional attachment, support, conversation, etc.). Also, some other factors could have been significant when it comes to a mother's behaviour (possible dysfunctional behaviour – smoking, alcohol, abuse, deprivation of any kind).

- **Chugani (1999):** This study used a PET scan of glucose metabolism of children aged 0–12 months. He explored what little activity in the cerebral cortex appeared. This activity in the brain stem and the thalamus is connected with inborn reflexes. The period between 6–9 months is very significant in the development of a baby's brain. Our memory and control of movements of the body are also improved because of the growth of the hippocampus and cerebellum. Children are now better adapted to the environment, can remember facts better and have bigger abilities to learn. Chugani also researched that glucose metabolism constantly increases in these areas of the brain. At this age the glucose metabolism is on the level of adult because of its increase (using the PET scan). Finally, the whole process that is called pruning takes place because of synaptic connections, which helps the baby to learn and keep synapses that are used and also expel those which are useless. In summary, from 1–12 months glucose metabolism changes in different areas of the brain (first in sensory and motor cortex, than parietal, temporal and primary visual cortex at 2–4 months, and finally about 8–12 months frontal cortex comes into play). This study clearly shows that there is a significant association between changes in the brain (neuroplasticity) and acquiring new psychological functions in the first months of our life.

- Discussing this idea can help to identify some arguments: Brain imaging technologies are only correlational, and don't allow researchers to draw conclusions about cause-and-effect relationship; as many biological arguments (if used alone without environmental and cognitive factors) could be perceived reductionist. Some studies suggest a direct correlation between brain development and development as a learner and are supported by theory of cognitive development proposed by Jean Piaget. This theory suggests that children need to be biologically ready to **jump in** to the next stage of development.

5.
- Poverty is a state in which a person or community does not have the necessary means (also financial) to maintain a minimum standard of living.
- Risk factors tend to negatively affect children's development (substance abuse, malnutrition and psychological stress). Protective factors help children to develop effectively and also protect children from potential threats.
- **Dickerson & Popli (2014):** This study aimed to investigate the impact of brain development on cognitive abilities. Researchers used data from 8,700 members of the Millennium Cohort Study. Their results showed that children born in poverty have significantly lower cognitive ability test results at 3, 5 and 7 years

of age, and that continuous life in poverty in the early years has a negative impact on their cognitive development. For children who have lived in poverty for the first years, their cognitive development test results at age 7 were substantially lower than children who have never experienced poverty, even after controlling a wide range of parental traits and investments. What is more, authors claim that poverty affects parental behaviour in a negative way. It results in a lack of time for everyday chores, lack of positive environment, and a struggle when trying to help children with their school chores. It seems that poverty has both direct and indirect influence on children's cognitive development. This study was longitudinal with the use of qualitative and quantitative research methods (method triangulation was used, which increases credibility of this study).

- **Luby et al. (2013):** In this study, researchers studied the role of poverty and parental skills in the changes in the brain structure. 145 children from 6–12 years of age took part in the study; their brains were scanned using MRI. It seemed that white matter (grey matter of children whose parents had not well-developed nurturing skills) grew significantly slower (especially in parts of the brain responsible for cognitive function, e.g. the hippocampus and amygdala). The findings that exposure to early childhood poverty has a significant impact on school-age brain development illustrates the importance of potential harmful effects of poverty on child development. These effects on the hippocampus are mediated by care and stressful life events.

- **Criticisms**: Most of terms are very vague and difficult to measure and operationalize (poverty). Different cultures have different GPA and there is a different perception of this phenomenon in different parts of the world. SES and poverty are significant factors in both a positive and negative way: having more money gives children more possibilities and better educational perspectives. Adverse childhood experiences play a role; however, it doesn't mean that children from less-privileged environments can't succeed.

- **Bhoomika's (2008):** This study investigated the role of malnutrition in the context of cognitive development. The results indicate that a correlation between these two exists. 20 Indian children were divided into two groups: 5–7 years and 8–10 years. The results were compared with a control group. Malnourished children in both age groups scored lower in attention tests, working memory tests and visuospatial tasks. Poverty is often linked to malnutrition.

- When it comes to studies, most of them are correlational, so no cause-and-effect can be identified. On the other hand, these studies are longitudinal, so the consequences of poverty can be clearly visible throughout the years. It's also important to conduct cross-cultural research to increase validity and possibility of generalization. When it comes to methodology, confounding variables could potentially affect the process of the study and results if researchers don't control them. To discuss the topic effectively one needs to think about different factors influencing cognitive development to present a more eclectic approach. Additionally, poverty can also affect other areas of our functioning (such as emotional wellbeing or physical health).

6.
- **Gender identity** is the perception of oneself as male, female or neither.
- Very important aspect of gender identity is gender roles which are external expectations about behaviour consistent/inconsistent with one's biological sex.
- **Kohlberg (1966):** In Kohlberg's theory gender development happens through three stages:
  - Gender labelling (around 2 years of age): children are able to identify themselves as boy or girl, but they also believe that gender is not constant, meaning it changes every time our physical appearance changes
  - Gender stability (around 4 years of age): children understand that gender is not a variable, meaning that boys will grow up to be a man and a girl will become a woman in the future
  - Gender consistency (5–7 years of age): understanding that gender doesn't change over time and is consistent regardless of your appearance or situation.

When a child gets older she/he has an idea that gender is unchanging; this idea, however, gradually changes into knowledge that one's gender is impossible to change.

- **Money and Erhardt (1972):** The researchers claimed that children were born gender neutral. According to Money, biological sex did not have to correspond to physiological sex (gender), and therefore children could be raised successfully in whatever sex was assigned to them. He was working with the Reimer family in Canada which had identical twin boys. Due to an accident, one of the boys lost his penis. Money used it as an opportunity to find support for his theory and told the parents to change the sex of the boy through surgery and hormone replacement, and raise him as a girl (Brenda). Money assumptions were not accurate. Brenda was not acting as a girl and was very unhappy and different from other girls. Eventually, at the age of 15, the parents told her the truth and Brenda became David again. This study showed that biology plays a key role in gender identity and is a counterargument towards Kohlberg's theory. It seriously contradicts the biosocial theory that socialization can replace biological makeup.

- **Criticism:** There was a set of ethical issues in this study. First of all, neither the twins nor their parents gave an informed consent to the twins being in a study. Lack of knowledge of the study means that they were not informed of their right to withdrawal. Also in the publications, Money revealed the case and identity of the twins, which violates the family's right to confidentiality. Finally the experiment caused mental harm to David who, for a large portion of his life, believed he was a girl. The study clearly presented confirmation bias as Money published information which confirmed his hypothesis. This case study as a research method doesn't let generalized findings relate to bigger population as every human being is unique and so are the circumstances.

- **Slaby & Frey (1975):** This study supported Kohlberg's theory and investigated the role of gender constancy among 2–5-year-old children; they conducted correlational research with the use of interviews. Children were interviewed about their gender constancy. After that, they were shown a movie where men and women were engaged in different activities. Children who showed stronger gender constancy during interviews were more interested in same-sex models. This finding is in line with Kohlberg's theory which claims that cognitive factors coexist with social factors in development of gender identity. Increasing gender constancy lead to selective observation of same sex models.

- **Evaluation of the theory:** Kohlberg's theory is based on Piaget's theory of cognitive development, so the evidence which supports Piaget's theory supports Kohlberg's as well. Research about gender schema theory claim that children who are about 3 years old get the information about gender consistent behaviours as they become their gender identity. Another argument is that this theory is mainly descriptive, but doesn't focus on an explanation of specific phenomenon. There is a question about the stages, as children could get through them earlier on, but because they are young their inability to communicate with others means it can't be verbalized. A very important consideration is that this theory assumes that every child experiences these stages at the same age and in the same order; however, all children are unique and can have a different understanding of gender roles/identity. They also are influenced by different environments and cultures. Cross-cultural studies should be performed to investigate difference between different countries, as well as similarities. When it comes to research methods used by Kohlberg (interviews) some children could give answers which they thought were expected from researchers.

7. • **A risk factor** is any feature, trait or situation of a person that increases the chance of developing an illness.
   - **A protective factor** stands for external and/or internal factor which allow people to cope with potential illness or stressful situations.
   - A health problem discussed will be stress.
   - **Selye (1956):** As Hans Selye wrote, stress is a failure to respond appropriately to emotional and physical threats. There are three main components: physiological (reaction of our body), cognitive (how we perceive the situation, as well as our cognitive symptoms), behavioural (how we react to stressful events, what do we do in response to stress).
   - **Cohen (1991):** The aim of the study was to investigate the role of psychological stress as a risk factor in infections. Participants were given questionnaires (Likert scale) to assess psychological stress, the effectiveness of their coping strategies, as well as emotional attitude towards them. After that 394 healthy people were given nasal drops containing one of five mild cold viruses, quarantined and monitored for infection symptoms. Participants who experienced negative life situations a couple of weeks before were twice as likely to catch cold in comparison with participants who experienced less psychological stress.

- **Evaluation of the study:** This study is interesting and informative; however, it doesn't explain how our body's ability to cope with disease changes because of stress. It used a questionnaire (self-assessment method) as a way of providing data about participants experience and attitude; this information can be biased as participants were subjective and may have wanted to look better as they were taking part in the study. When it comes to procedure, most of the participants showed some signs of illness; however, not all of them were told that they had a cold – mild deception was used. It is also somewhat unethical to expose participants to cold viruses; however, not seriously dangerous. Researchers were able to control potential confounding variables (e.g. age, gender, smoking, allergies, weight, alcohol, diet and exercise). The sample size was relatively big, which increases the possibility of generalization of findings. It is also important that stress is very subjective, so people could assess their stress levels as higher/lower depending on individual differences.

- **Dolbier et al. (2007):** The aim of this study was to investigate the effectiveness of a resilience intervention as a protective factor. 57 college students were randomly assigned to two groups (experimental or control). Experimental group took part in intervention sessions (four sessions were each focused on a different aspect: typical responses to stress, taking responsibility, focusing and empowering interpretations, creating meaningful connections). They completed a survey about resilience, coping strategies, protective factors, and symptomatology before and after sessions. The findings of this study indicate that the experimental group had significantly higher resilience scores, more effective coping strategies (more effective problem-solving strategies), higher scores on protective factors (i.e. optimism, positive affect, higher self-esteem and self-leadership), and lower scores on symptomatology (i.e., depressive symptoms, negative affect and perceived stress).
   - **Evaluation of the study:** It refers to a well-established transactional model of stress and coping by **Lazarus and Folkman (1984)** so it has a solid theoretical background. The sample of the study was diverse (Caucasian, Asian, Hispanic and African American). Many other studies investigated the effectiveness of stress-management programmes with results showing stress reduction and health improvement. Participants were compensated for taking part in the study as researchers found it difficult to find participants for their study. Researchers used surveys which can provide biased answers due to social desirability bias or inability of accurate self-assessment. Research method triangulation (qualitative and/or qualitative) could be used in future studies to address this limitation. The sample was relatively small so more diverse and larger group should be taken under consideration in future studies. There was no random sampling of participants from a population, which affects possible generalization and external validity of the study. Future research could focus on different long-term effects of stress coping strategies.

8. • One health problem used in this response will be obesity. The studies used will be Lombard et al. (2012) & Haworth et al. (2008), with the biological explanation being genes.
   - Obesity occurs when a person carries excessive weight. This puts them at greater risk for a number of diseases.
   - There are many factors which contribute as a cause of this health problem (obesity). Most of them are controlled by humans (diet, exercise, sedentary lifestyle); however, biological explanation plays a role as well (e.g. genes). But analysing this approach alone would be reductionist.
   - **Lombard et al. (2012):** The aim was to check the correlation between genes and obesity using body mass index (BMI). Researchers performed a longitudinal study with participants being 990 South Africans; their BMI was assessed as well as their genetic history. Weight, height, sex, sex-specific puberty stage and exact age was collected during puberty (13 years) and used to identify loci predisposed to obesity early in life. Four genes were individually significantly associated with BMI. Each gene was linked with an estimated average 2.5% increase of BMI.
   - **Haworth (2008):** The researchers used a twin study to investigate heritability of BMI and obesity. The study used UK participants of around 2,300 same sex pairs of 7 year olds, and over 3,500 same-sex pairs of 10 year olds. Parents filled out questionnaires and provided information about height and weight of the children. With reference to their BMI, children were assigned to different groups (overweight, obese and normal weight). The twin method

was applied to identify BMI correlations between monozygotic (MZ) twins, then compared to BMI associations between dizygotic (DZ) twins. Researchers focused on environment as well. Regardless of age, the study showed that genetic inheritance played a major role in BMI and obesity (60%–74%), whereas environment played a role in 12%–22%. The results of this study show that obesity is significant genetically determined.

- **To evaluate the biological explanation**, critical analysis of studies is needed. Genetic studies in general don't let a researcher identify cause-and-effect relationships, as these are only correlational; experiments are needed to ensure direct relationships exist between variables. Lombard's study used a long-term approach to identify changes in the long run which is a strength. Genetic approach also should be analysed cross culturally to know the possible cultural influences in terms of obesity. Taking genetic explanation under consideration, one also needs to remember that results of these two studies don't determine this approach as solely responsible for obesity (2.5% increase in the first study and 60%–74% in the second means that there other factors which play a role as well) to use an eclectic, not reductionist approach. In a genetic approach using twin studies, one needs to remember that the MZ and DZ twins will have similar environments; this is one of the benefits of studying DZ twins, not just ordinary siblings. This assumption means that stronger phenotypic similarity to MZ is linked to genetic factor. If this is the case, MZ twins experience more similar environments than DZ twins, and then phenotypic similarity could derive from environmental rather than genetic factors. It can lead to a conclusion that more attention should be put to gene-environment interaction, which assumes that genes and environmental influences together lead to development of obesity. Twin studies are not representative of the general population so generalization is limited due to environmental influences.

9. • **Health promotion** refers to any strategies/programmes which aim is to encourage health-related behaviour by implementing different actions (education, mass media, interpersonal).

- **Horne (2004):** This investigated healthy eating among British primary school children with the use of peer modelling and rewards. Researchers used about 750 children aged 5–11 from London. The amount of fruits and vegetables was measured at the beginning of the study so that potential difference would be clearly visible after research is done. Experimental and control school was engaged in the study. For 5 months children in both schools were given a choice of fruits and vegetables for lunch. Younger children (5–7) were given fruits during a snack time. Additionally (for 16 days) in experimental school children watched videos about Food Dudes – imaginary teenage superheroes who eat healthy themselves and try to prevent the world from eating junk food. At the same time they talk a lot about what makes them so strong and invincible (fruits and vegetables, of course) also how tasty and beneficial these are. Researchers measured the amount of vegetables and fruits after the intervention using the 5-point scale. Results showed that there was a significant difference in the level of fruit and vegetable consumption both at school and at home. The study clearly shows the change in healthy eating habits in children by implementation of social cognitive theory by Bandura. This theory is based on observational learning and modelling especially at the young age.
  - **Ethical considerations in this study are** informed consent and the use of children as participants of the study; parents need to be aware of the study and sign the agreement as children were under 16. They also need to know what the study is about. Right to withdraw is another issue – if parents don't want their children to take part in this kind of programme because they think they are responsible for children's eating habits there should be a chance to withdraw at any time, as well as withdrawal of the data after the study is over. Anonymity is another very important factor as results shouldn't be published with the use of sensitive details. This can potentially lead to stigmatization after the study if it turns out that some children didn't change their level of healthy eating.
- Fear appeal consists of three parts: fear, threat and efficacy. Fear is a negatively balanced emotion that is usually accompanied by heightened psychological arousal. Threat is an external stimulus that creates a perception in message receivers that they are susceptible to some negative situation or outcome. And perceived efficacy is a person's belief that message recommendations can be implemented and will effectively reduce the threat depicted in the message **(Williams (2012): Gore et al. (1998))**.

- **Akyuz (2014):** This investigated the fear appeal in anti-smoking campaigns. Researcher used questionnaires to gather data with independent samples: 396 smokers and non-smokers took part in the study. Students answered questions after watching advertisements provided by Public Service called *Smoking is Regret*. First questions were asked about the level of interest towards PSA. Smokers didn't show interest towards anti-smoking advertisements compared with non-smokers; the same result was regarding the effectiveness of PSAs. The results show that there are two factors which are significant in stopping smoking: the financial burden of smoking and the belief that smoking affects attractiveness negatively (yellow teeth and nails, smell, general perception of people). Women are more concerned about the look-deteriorating effects of smoking. So the results clearly show that addiction makes cigarette users non-responsive towards negative health consequences. However, they are aware of the health risks of using cigarettes but they do not want to hear about them. So it seems that fear appeal advertisements are not effective in stimulating the behaviour of cigarette users. If the emphasis would be on negative consequences in the context of attractiveness, especially among women, then these could be more effective. To sum up, fear appeal programmes resulted in less-positive attitude towards recommendations; intentions to engage in healthy activities were not strong as well.

- **Ethical issue in this study** is focused on psychological harm specifically, as fear appeal in public health campaigns is widely discussed. Fear appeal is based on negative emotions and potential threat towards potential victims. Studies show this doesn't make campaigns more effective unless these are focused on positive outcomes and/or self-efficacy specifically. Most of such campaigns and studies that investigate them, target victims, not potential users or health problems, so the level of effectiveness in prevention is questionable. There is a wide debate if fear appeal actually motivates people to stop smoking, as studies show in many cases these are ineffective. Psychological harm in this kind of study can be caused when people imagine themselves suffering from serious health conditions caused by unhealthy behaviour (smoking) as it can potentially change their attitude and make them more aware. And so exposing them in specific studies to these kinds of scenarios and/or pictures is somewhat unethical. Knowledge of the dangers of smoking will not change the behaviours of smokers.

10. • Different factors and theories are developed to understand the process of creating relationships. One of the important factors is communication, which is significant in different aspects of our life. It can affect our attraction, level of trust towards a partner, how stressed we are or it can potentially lead to a change or end of a relationship.

- **Altman & Taylor (1973):** This study came up with the social penetration theory. It says that humans have a tendency to carefully choose people when sharing very personal and intimate information. As the relationship changes (develops) the type of exchange is also different. It becomes intimate and emotional, based on feelings. In many cases we also analyse some inner doubts. This tendency is bigger when it comes to people we trust and like. It seems that self-disclosure is a significant factor in personal relationships, as it is based on effective communication between partners.

- **Fincham & O'Leary (1983):** This study examined attributions in the context of human relationships. 37 couples in total took part in the study (18 distressed couples taking part in marital therapy and 19 non-distressed couples who responded to a local advertisement). All of them had been married for at least a couple of years. All participants were asked to fill in questionnaires about marital adjustment and areas of difficulty, as well as attributions for difficulties. Some of the questions asked to indicate the extent to which the cause of the difficulty rested on themselves, the partner, the relationship itself, or outside circumstances. Distressed spouses, in comparison to non-distressed spouses, were more likely to see their partner and the relationship as the source of the marital difficulties – these would be dispositional (controllable) factors. What is more, distressed couples viewed positive behaviours as uncontrollable (situational). This seems to confirm attribution theory – that we have a tendency to explain different behaviours by using different types of attribution. It is very important in the context of communication and personal relationships as it is closely related to self-disclosure, trust and empathy between partners. There is a concern that negative situations in marriage can lead to a change in attribution – the question is: if this is a process or a fixed state of relationship.

- **Gottman & Levenson (1986):** The results of the study indicate that misunderstandings and anger exchanges relate to unhappiness and negative interactions at home; at the same time, on the other hand, predicted longitudinal improvement in marital satisfaction. However, three interaction patterns were identified as dysfunctional in terms of longitudinal deterioration: defensive (which includes whining), stubbornness, and withdrawal from interaction. All of them are directly linked to communication patterns.
  - Gottmann identified Four Horsemen of Apocalypse, based on many years of observations, interviews and questionnaires in his institute. The theory is mainly based on common negative communication patterns within relationships.
  - **Criticism:** The first factor is based on the dispositional attribution (attacking one's character and not the behaviour). The second is defensiveness (a tendency to defend oneself and blame others). Third is contempt (lack of respect, sarcasm, eye rolling). Fourth is stonewalling (not engaging in conversation and ignoring your spouse, a very significant predictor of divorce).
- **Critical thinking about the topic:** Social penetration theory is based on self-disclosure; the term is very broad and subjective; in many cases data is gathered through self-assessment methods. Communication in general is hard to study and to operationalize – as many couples have their own ways of conversation. In long-lasting relationships there could be an issue with memory distortion and routine; some information could be forgotten or taken for granted. When focusing on distressed partners it is often not possible to get the full picture of a situation; the study should be longitudinal to observe the progress/changes within the relationship over time. When it comes to Gottman's theory, there is a possibility of researcher bias and demand characteristics, as expectations from both sides could potentially affect the behaviour and its interpretation. There are differences in communication when it comes to gender. It is also important to look at possible cultural differences in communication between partners; to address this limitation researchers should conduct cross-cultural studies. Also taking only one factor under consideration (self-disclosure or communication) is not enough as many other factors could potentially affect relationships. Taking attribution styles and other factors all together can eventually lead to valid conclusions.

11. • **Howarth (2002):** Researchers performed eight focus groups (people knew each other quite well) with 44 teenagers aged 12–16 as participants. Interviews were also done with high school principals in Brixton. The questions asked were: what is it like to live in Brixton and what people outside Brixton think about Brixton. Thematic guidelines were used to make sure that questions about the community, social inclusion, exclusion, identity, ethnicity, media, prejudice, racism and schools were included. After interviews, Howarth conducted a thematic analysis and the emerging topics included the role of the media, the role of the family, the belief that Brixton is black and the presence of self-hatred. Howarth noted that the very negative representation of 'being from Brixton' by people outside this area was not shared by all the people living there. Some participants said that their community members were 'diverse, creative and spontaneous', which is a different view for most bystanders. The results of the study confirmed the theory of social identity.
  - **Evaluation:** A focus group (five people in the group) was a research method used in this study with purposive sampling. This research method is effective as it's a relatively quick and easy way to gather data from many participants; however it is not always accurate for sensitive topics. The use of questionnaires could also be a good idea as an even more convenient and quick way to get information from participants. Additionally, interviews were done with school principals so data triangulation was used to increase credibility. On the other hand, conformity could have affected the participant's answers during the interview. Other people can also be a trigger for some ideas and opinions about the topic which is a strength.
- **Scherif (1954):** The illustration of RCT and cooperation (Robber's Cave experiment) the aim was to investigate informal groups and dynamic processes among them (e.g. conflict/cooperation). Participants were of similar age (11–12), came from the middle class and were also connected by the fact that they were all white Protestants. The experiment consisted of three stages. In the first, the boys were divided into two teams. Each of them, unaware of the existence of the second group, was transported to Robbers Cave and gradually created their own internal norms. The participants discovered the area, were playing, swimming and climbing together; they also came up with names for their teams (Rattlers and Eagles). The next step was to create opportunities for interaction between groups. After a week, the Rattlers and Eagles met for the first time. Within a few days, both teams measured each other in a series of agility tasks and games. The scoring caused the first friction; with each subsequent task, the competition got sharper and the relations between the teams peaked faster and faster. The experimenters decided that each time, the victory of one team would be associated with the lack of a prize for the second team. The boys refused to eat together. After losing the competition, the Eagles stole and set fire to their rivals' flag. Rattlers demolished the opponents' hut in revenge. Representatives of the groups treated each other with increasing hostility; the first fights and racist insults appeared. The researchers asked the participants to evaluate both groups – the boys were very negative towards the rivals, at the same time being positive towards their own surroundings. The last phase of the experiment is (after a momentary separation) the group meeting again. This time, the tasks imposed by the researchers required cooperation. Not all of the activities proposed by Sherif and colleagues proved effective to reconcile the warring parties. Only the feeling of danger for both groups, for which the Eagles and Rattlers could not blame each other, was successful. While both groups were together, the researchers damaged the water tank. The risk of failure of the summer camp and the necessity of taking quick actions meant that both teams went hand in hand to work with a common goal. Leaving Robbers Cave, Rattlers and Eagles were not enemies. They had a joint success, and their mutual relationships (strengthened by subsequent tasks arranged by the Sherif team) had improved significantly. Superordinate goals helped both groups to work together.
- The research method used was a field experiment, which means that the study was done in a natural environment (high ecological validity as the study was based on summer camp and involved common activities), but researchers didn't have control over extraneous variables that could potentially affect the study and the results (internal validity could be lower). Participants didn't know the true aim of this experiment, so demand characteristic was unlikely to appear. However, not directly connected to RM, the sample was small and biased with only 12-year-old American boys taking part in the study. This experiment was also ethnocentric. Another methodological consideration is the influence of researcher biases on the results of a study. If researchers had their own opinion about the progress or results of the Robber's Cave experiment it could potentially affect the results of the study or interpretations.

12. • **Bystanderism** is a situation in which a witness of a critical situation chooses not to help the victim because other people are also present in the same situation.
- One of the theories which tries to explain this phenomenon is the theory of unresponsive behaviour by **Latane & Darley (1970)**. Another significant factor is diffusion of responsibility (being in a group of people observing an event diminishes the level of responsibility of individual witnesses), as well as pluralistic ignorance (one's tendency to observe and follow the reactions of other people when deciding what to do in a specific situation).
- **Latane & Darley (1968):** 59 people (students from New York University) were asked to exchange opinions on the personal problems of student life and adaptation to the new environment. To ensure anonymity, each person was in a separate room. With the help of microphone headphones, each person was to share their thoughts with others who apparently were in the neighbouring rooms. The participants were divided into three groups: group 1 spoke to one person, group 2 to two, and group 3 to five. Each participant was alone and the voices were played from the tape. The critical situation occurred when the participants after a conversation with their partner, suddenly heard the information about the partner being unwell. Participants were told that the neighbour was suffering from epilepsy and was about to have a seizure. Immediately after this statement, the interlocutor's voice collapsed and choking noises started. There was also a cry for help. The respondents got 4 minutes to react (leave the room and inform the experimenters). When the reaction did not occur, the

experiment was over. The results of the study showed that when the witnesses were sure that they were the only observers, the chance that they would help was high (85%), the reaction occurred quickly (52 seconds). If the respondent was aware that he/she was not alone, the probability of providing help decreased (62%) and the response time increased (93 seconds). The least chance of help was when there were three or more witnesses (then 31% of participants helped in approximately 100 seconds). The result of the experiment confirmed the hypothesis: the more witnesses, the less willingness to help. It also illustrated two factors from the theory of unresponsive behaviour: diffusion of responsibility and pluralistic ignorance.

- The results of this study are also confirmed by **Latane & Darley (1969)** in their experiment. In the room where the experiment was taking place, smoke began to come out. The researchers investigated after how long the participants would react depending on the size of the group in which they were; other members would pretend not to notice the smoke. 55% of the respondents, being alone in the room, reported the appearance of smoke within 2 minutes, while in the other, larger groups, only 12% did. After 4 minutes, 75% of alone participants took action, while none of the other groups did so. The fact that this piece of research illustrated the given theory, as well as other studies confirming the results of this study, are strengths of this research. As this was an experiment, there was a control over potential confounding variables (the study was done in a laboratory); also there were three groups. On the other hand, the study was artificial as the experiment presented the situation which is not likely to happen in everyday life. What is more, the sample (students) are highly motivated and easily available (which is a strength); however, they could potentially have a knowledge about the study or try to guess the aim of the experiment and act accordingly (a limitation). The number of people is small (59) so the possibility of generalization is limited. Also the sample was biased as the participants were students taken from one university. Some ethical concerns are also visible in this study: participants were deceived as they were not told the true aim of the study and no informed consent was given to them. Also after being debriefed, participants could feel uncomfortable with their behaviour, which potentially could cause self-doubt and affect self-esteem (psychological harm).

- **Irving and Jane Piliavin (1969)** decided to investigate Arousal Cost Reward Model (ACRM). It is mainly based on the assumption that the reason why we decide to help other people is slightly egoist – we want to reduce negative feelings. When we feel bad in one negative situation, the next step would be to think about the cost of helping/not helping. If the cost outweighs the benefits we decide not to engage in helping behaviour.
  - The study was done as a field experiment in New York subway with the use of opportunity sampling. About 4,450 men and women travelling for 7.5 minutes between two stations took part in the study. The main purpose of the study was to influence the type of victim (drunk or sick) and race of the victim (black or white) on response speed, response frequency and the race of the helper. 103 trials were done. Four victims were young men (26 and 35 years old, three white and one black). They were dressed identically. In 38 trials, victims smelled of alcohol and had an alcohol bottle tightly wrapped in a brown bag (drunk), while in the remaining 65 trials they looked sober and had a black cane (sober). The victim with the cane received spontaneous help in 62 out of 65 attempts. The person in a drunk condition received spontaneous help in 19 of 38 trials. There was a difference in the time taken to help in both conditions: the median of 5 seconds in sober condition and 109 seconds in drunken condition. According to ACRM, people were considering costs and benefits longer before acting as the decision could have been more potentially dangerous. It is interesting to note that 90% of helpers were male. There was no difference in helping when it came to black and white people. The frequency of help received by the victims was impressive compared to the results from other laboratory studies.

- **Evaluation of the study:** It seems difficult to compare results from studies done in the natural environment and laboratory – they seem contradictory (especially in this case). Some ethical issues as well – it is not comfortable to see someone collapsing on the train (possible psychological harm); deception – participants were not aware that the whole situation was a fake, they didn't agree to take part in the study (no informed consent); they were not

debriefed as they got off the train, so they didn't have a chance to withdraw their data. As a field experiment done in a natural environment there is high ecological validity, but on the other hand there was no possibility to control confounding variables that could have affected the study and its results. Also the place of the study could potentially affect the results as there could be some potential set of characteristics of people travelling by subway. Additionally, most of the helpers were male, as well as the victims. The study was done in the USA (generalization is limited) and sampling technique and sampling bias could be an issue.

Set B: Paper 3 (HL)

1a. • Covert participant observation.
- One characteristic of this research method is that participants don't know they are being observed by researchers.
- Another factor is that there could be an issue of objectivity, as researchers became part of the cult (they could try to justify cult members' behaviour or develop close relationships with them).

1b. • Opportunity sampling was used in this study.
- This sampling method focuses on an already existing group of people. In this study, researchers were investigating people being members of a cult.
- The problem with this sampling method in this case is that the sample is not highly representative to the general population or other outside circumstances.

1c. • Focus groups: small group interviews with cult members could provide insight into their way of thinking and help justify the decision-making process. However, it would need to be done in an overt way and people would know that they are in the study, which could potentially result in demand characteristics or psychological harm (self-doubt).

2. • Participants were not informed about the observation being conducted (informed consent was not provided).
- As covert participant observation was used, deception had to be used to ensure lack of reactivity and natural behaviour. However, it was unethical not to inform participants that they were taking part in the study and that new cult members were actually researchers.
- The data of cult members should remain anonymous.
- Participants of this covert observation should be debriefed after the study is finished.
- They also should have a chance to withdraw their data after debriefing.
- Psychological harm could also be an issue after debriefing – if cult members became aware of being lied to by fake fellow members it could lead to negative emotions, which can cause lower self-esteem and self-doubt (in terms of how accurate and justified their decisions were).
- Lack of objectivity, researcher bias (confirmation bias), too personal involvement, memory-distortion. Reflexivity and triangulation could be used to deal with mentioned biases:
  - Reflexivity would help to control (increase an awareness) possible beliefs/attitudes towards the whole study or cult members.
  - Researcher triangulation would address possible subjectivity when analysing behaviours or interpreting results, as well as too personal involvement in hypothetical social situations during the observation. Asking other researchers to observe the same thing could deal with memory distortion while making notes.

3. Lack of objectivity, researcher bias (confirmation bias), too personal involvement and memory distortion – reflexivity and triangulation could be used to deal with mentioned biases. Reflexivity would help to control (increase an awareness) possible beliefs/attitudes towards the whole study or cult members. Researcher triangulation would address possible subjectivity when analysing behaviors or interpreting results, as well as too personal involvement in hypothetical social situations during the observation. Asking other researchers to observe the same thing could deal with memory distortion while making notes.

Set C: Paper 1 (SL and HL): Section A

1. • **A hormone** is a biochemical produced by the glands of the endocrine system, which is transported by the bloodstream to specific cells and organs in the body in order to initiate specific biological responses. The endocrine system is a system comprised of glands, which secrete hormones into the bloodstream to affect behaviour. From there, the hormones are sent to target cells by impulses that initiate specific responses. The human body can produce a large number of hormones, many of which have a large influence on our emotions and behaviour. Common examples are adrenaline, testosterone and oxytocin.

- **Oxytocin** is produced in the hypothalamus and released by the pituitary gland. It plays a role in sexual reproduction and social bonding. A study on this hormone was conducted by **Kosfeld et al. (2005)**. The aim was to prove that oxytocin increases trust in humans. He designed a trust game in which participants were paired anonymously and played the role of either an investor or trustee. He gathered 128 male students and allocated them randomly into groups with an oxytocin or placebo group. Substances were administered via an intranasal spray. Each round of the game had three steps based on sending monetary units between an investor and trustee. Participants played the game four times, each time paired with another person and in the end the earned monetary units were exchanged for real money. Results of the experiment showed that the level of trust in those participants who received a dose of oxytocin was higher than in the placebo group. The median transfer of investors was higher in the oxytocin group than the control group. 45% of the oxytocin group showed maximum trust level exchanging whole sums of monetary units. The researchers suggested two explanations to these findings: oxytocin reduces risk of aversion and oxytocin increases people's trust in others. They later clarified that oxytocin a plays role specifically in interpersonal interactions.
- The researchers concluded that oxytocin can influence people's willingness to put trust in others. The participants had to overcome the aversion towards the risk. Either way, both explanations stated in the end of the study prove that the hormone affects human behaviour, whether it is trust or overcoming aversion. Also, the study relates to the function of oxytocin as it is responsible for social bonding. However, because the researchers tested only a male group the findings cannot be simply generalized. The study refers to the simplistic view that oxytocin leads to easier bonding between humans, as it is called 'the love hormone', in that way it could be explained that it stirs some aspects of human behaviour: being more trusting and sociable. The effect of oxytocin on human behaviour is supported by the valid study done by **Kosfeld et al. (2005)**, which proves its influence. Nevertheless, it is not appropriate to say that hormones 'cause' behaviour, rather that hormones change the probability that a particular behaviour will be displayed. Therefore, hormones simply influence behaviour.

2. • **Schemas** – or mental representations of knowledge – are based on previous experiences and human memory. Different types of schemas (for example, self-schemas, scripts and social schemas) help us to make sense of the world around us. We learn what behavior is or isn't appropriate. Schemas could also be changed throughout our life. *Self-schemas* refer to us (what we know about ourselves like our strengths/weaknesses); *scripts* are about situations or skills (what to do and how to do it); *social schemas* more generally refer to groups of people and how we perceive them (such as stereotypes).
- Humans are information processors, this is why we actively gain and recall information (by encoding and retrieval), we tend to implement existing knowledge into new information. Jean Piaget (the author of the Theory of Cognitive Development) explained assimilation and accommodation in terms of how schemas are created: Assimilation happens when new information needs to be changed (adjusted) to fit an existing schema; accommodation is when the existing schema is not accurate and needs to be modified because of the existence of some new information.
- **Frederic Bartlett (1932)** investigated schemas in his study entitled: 'The War of the Ghost'. Bartlett aimed to determine how social and cultural factors influence schemas and hence can lead to memory distortions.

Method:
- Participants used were of an English background.
- They were asked to read 'The War of the Ghosts' – a Native American folk tale.
- Tested their memory of the story using serial reproduction and repeated reproduction, where they were asked to recall it six or seven times over various retention intervals.
  - Serial reproduction: the first participant reading the story reproduces it on paper, which is then read by a second participant who reproduces the first participant's

reproduction, and so on until it is reproduced by six or seven different participants.
  - Repeated reproduction: the same participant reproduces the story six or seven times from their own previous reproductions. Their reproductions occur between time intervals from 15 minutes to as long as several years.

Results:
Both methods lead to similar results.
- As the number of reproductions increased, the story became shorter and there were more changes to the story. For example, 'hunting seals' changed into 'fishing' and 'canoes' became 'boats'.
- These changes show the alteration of culturally unfamiliar things into what the English participants were culturally familiar with.
- This makes the story more understandable according to the participants' experiences and cultural background (schemas).
- Results indicated that recalled stories were distorted and altered in various ways making it more conventional and acceptable to their own cultural perspective (rationalization).
- Memory is reconstructive and based on pre-existing schemas. Bartlett's study helped to explain through the understanding of schemas when people remember stories, they typically omit ('leave out') some details, and introduce rationalizations and distortions, because they reconstruct the story so as to make more sense in terms of their knowledge, the culture in which they were brought up in and experiences in the form of schemas. Bartlett's study shows how schema theory is useful to understand how people categorize information, interpret stories, and make inferences. It also contributes to the understanding of cognitive distortions in memory.

3. • **Acculturation** is a process of psychological and cultural change as a result of contact and interaction between different cultures. It can lead to changes to all cultures, not only one. This statement was wrought by **Berry (2005)**. Acculturation differs from enculturation as it means internalizing norms of the dominant culture one migrated to, where enculturation means internalizing the norms of one's own culture of origin. Individuals can adopt four strategies of cultural change. Each one is a combination of two independent dimensions: maintenance of heritage culture and seeking relationships with other groups. The study conducted by **Ishikawa and Jones (2016)** explored acculturation and health behaviour of migrants.
- The experiment analysed obesity in Asian migrants in the United States of America. They assumed that there are some protective factors that can serve as a buffer against developing obesity in migrants. The aim was to compare obesity rates among second and third generation Asian migrants in the USA and to identify potential moderating factors of developing obesity. The research method used in the study was correlational research. The results showed that second- and third-generation migrants had a higher likelihood of obesity in comparison to first-generation ones or people from their country of origin. However, there were moderating factors that protected against developing obesity, such as: living in a neighbourhood with a high migrant density or in a household that retained the original language. It showed that retaining some ties with the original culture may serve as a protective factor against developing obesity in migrants. The results are formulated in terms of causation, that is moderating factors that protect against obesity, but we should remember that it is still just an inference. The conclusion that retaining the original language protects form developing obesity seems plausible but is not certain.
- **As in any correlational study**, there could be other factors influencing the association of the variables. Limitation of the method is the problem that correlations themselves cannot be interpreted as causations. In this way it is not possible to find the real cause of obesity in Asian migrants. This means that it is impossible to claim that one co-variable actually causes the other co-variable, as it could be that a third unknown variable (a mediating variable) is causing both variables to change together. As a result, correlational studies cannot provide conclusive information about causal relationships among variables. Only experimental research designs in which the independent variable is manipulated by the experimenter can do this.
- **As for the strength of correlational study** – it focuses on a naturally occurring situation as no variables are manipulated (in some cases the manipulation of IV which potentially could affect the dependent variable would be not ethical), so ecological validity is high, which means that the same situation can happen in the future on an everyday basis.

Set C: Paper 1 (SL and HL): Section B

4. • Genetic information is stored in the human body in our DNA, and the expression of these genes triggers a certain set of amino acids that regulate physical traits, brain function, and behaviour, among others. More so, the increased or decreased expression of a certain gene also affects human behaviour, and it is a concept researchers have been trying to prove by studying the expression of certain genes and how it leads to changes in behaviour.

• Psychologists have taken an interest in how genes could influence behaviour and their influence can be seen in several studies, such as **Caspi et al. (2003)** and **Kendler et al. (2006)** who wanted to determine the role of genetics in developing depression.

• **Caspi et al. (2003)** conducted a longitudinal study to investigate the human behaviour of depression and how the 5-HTT gene was linked to it. The 5-HTT gene regulates the levels of serotonin in the synapse. Serotonin is a neurotransmitter that influences mood and is said to be linked to feelings of happiness and wellbeing. The aim of the study was to investigate whether afunctional change in the 5-HTT gene can lead to a higher or lower risk of depression in an individual. The sample was divided based on whether an individual had a short allele (mutation) of the 5-HTT gene or the standard long allele, which is slightly more frequent in humans (57%). The sample was an opportunity sample that it included 847 26 year olds from New Zealand who were divided into three groups; those with (1) two short alleles, (2) one short and one long allele, and (3) two long alleles. The participants filled in a survey about stressful life events from the past five years and were psychologically assessed for depression. The results were compared with the length of alleles in the individuals. The study found that the individuals who carried a mutation of the 5-HTT gene (groups 1 and 2) and experienced many stressful events were more likely to become depressed after stressful events than the participants who carried the longer version of 5-HTT gene.

• **Discussion:** Though the 5-HTT gene doesn't cause depression, the way it interacts with the environment of the individual – particularly during stressful situations – can increase the chances of the individual becoming depressed. The researchers were able to conclude that the mutation of the 5-HTT gene, which is responsible for the regulation of serotonin, creates a vulnerability to depression and that a mutation in the 5-HTT gene creates a genetic predisposition to depression. This shows that depression is due to both genetic and environmental factors and, therefore, is evidence of how a gene is linked to human behaviour. Also the study was correlational (no cause-and-effect relationship), and used self-reports which in turn could have affected the ability to recall negative life events. However, it is good because there is the acknowledgment of the coexistence of biological and environmental factors in the etiology of depression.

• **Kendler (2006):** Researchers wanted to investigate the possible difference between men and women in terms of heritability of depression, as well as checking the coexistence of genetic and environmental factors as potential causes of depression. Major lifetime depression was evaluated during telephone interviews based on modified DSM-IV criteria in 42,161 twins, including 15,493 full pairs, from the national register of the Swedish register of twins. Results showed that inheritance of responsibility for major depression was significantly higher in women (42%) than men (29%), and genetic risk factors for major depression were moderately correlated in men and women. In the largest sample, major depressive disorder was moderately hereditary, with estimates similar to those in previous studies. According to some, but not most previous investigations, this study suggests both that the inheritance of major depression is higher in women than in men, and that some genetic risk factors for major depression are gender specific.

• **Some critical arguments** towards this study are similar to the previous factors: self-assessment plus correlational study and a very big sample in this study was a strength, but the research method (telephone interviews) could have been flawed because of the lack of interpersonal contact with a clinician, memory distortions or demand characteristics.

• In general, genetic studies are quite reliable and consistent in findings. Many people can think the genetic argument could be reductionist; however, genes are affected by the environment (epigenetics) and also both of these factors work together to affect human behaviour (e.g. depression). One of limitations of genetics is the fact that twins, which are often chosen as a sample for studies, do not represent the whole population because of the obvious characteristics – generalization is limited. There is

also this consideration of cultural differences and genetics in the context of etiologies of mental illnesses, such as depression.

5. • **Emotion** remains one of the most difficult psychological concepts to define, due to its complexity. The most basic definition would be that it is a pattern of changes in the whole organism, which includes physical arousal, expressive behaviours and conscious experience. It is generally made in response to a situation perceived to be personally significant. In this essay the main focus will be on the two pieces of research (**Brown & Kulik (1977)** and **Neisser & Harsch (1992)**), which investigate the effect of emotions on memory formation and maintenance.

• The term flashbulb memory (FBM) was first introduced by researchers **Brown & Kulik**. According to them, FBM is a memory one has of the first time they learn about an unexpected and consequential (or emotionally arousing) event. It is not the memory of the event itself, but rather of its reception context.

• The researchers conducted a study in which they asked questions about ten events to a group of 80 people (40 white and 40 black). Nine of the events were mainly assassinations or attempted assassinations of well-known American personalities (e.g. John F. Kennedy or Martin Luther King). The tenth event was a personal one, of a similar nature – unexpected and of a high emotional relevance. The participants were asked to recall the circumstances in which they first learned about these events. They found out that 90% of the participants recalled learning about the assassination of John F. Kennedy in vivid detail. African Americans were more accurate when it came to assassinations of the leaders of civil rights movements (e.g. Martin Luther King) than Caucasian Americans. The personal event (e.g. learning about the death of a parent) was recalled in vivid detail by the majority of the participants. Since these events were both unexpected and personally relevant for the participants, it can be stated that the results were consistent with the FBM theory.

• On the other hand, there are numerous studies which question the FBM theory, one of them being the research by **Neisser and Harsch**. They asked a group of participants how they found out about the disaster of the spaceship *Challenger*. They did this twice: one day after the event and then 2.5 years later. To be sure, the researchers conducted semi-structured interviews after the second questionnaire was given. They found that one day after the disaster 21% of the participants claimed that they learned about it from TV. However, after 2.5 years this number rose up to 45%. Assuming that the participants were more accurate right after the disaster, their memories became highly distorted. This suggests that FBM are not very reliable. According to the findings of the study, FBM may be no different than ordinary, everyday memories.

• All of the above-mentioned studies can be presumed ecologically valid, as they related to real-life events, researchers didn't manipulate variables, and the study wasn't done under strictly controlled conditions. On the other hand, all of them, whether supporting or contradicting the FBM theory, have similar methodological issues. Firstly, they lacked a control group. None of them included asking the participants about an ordinary event that would happen around the same time as the highly emotional one. Therefore, a clear comparison between FBMs and ordinary memories was impossible. These studies were based on the assumption that flashbulb memories are a special, different kind of memory – an assumption that isn't necessarily true. Also, in the studies supporting Brown and Kulik's theory, there was really no certainty that what the participants recalled was true. The moment at which the participants learned about the investigated events was obviously not recorded in any way. Describing something in vivid detail isn't tantamount to recalling it the way it actually was (the questionnaires were retrospective). Therefore, we can't be sure whether the initial memory was accurate or already distorted by rehearsal. Also, the obvious limitation of both studies is that these can't be replicated.

• **Brown & Kulik study:** Social desirability bias could have affected the responses of participants as this was a very important situation for many individuals. As for the sample, American males took part in the study (sampling bias), which makes it difficult to generalize to other cultures and genders.

• **Neisser & Harsch study:** There was a lack of control over the behaviour of participants between the first and second questionnaire (no control over possible confounding variables which could have affected the memory of participants). A case study was used as a research method (it allows a deeper insight into the investigated phenomenon, also because of the use of method triangulation) and in contrast with Brown & Kulik's study it was a prospective study. As the most important thing was to observe the changes of memories over time, this study was done longitudinally.

6. • A stereotype is a belief about a group of people. The role of stereotypes can be both beneficial and negative. On one hand, these can help us to make a sense of the world as the thinking process is very quick, which leads to quick decisions and responses based on our previous experiences (schemas). On the other hand, stereotypes make us ignore other important factors or characteristics about people; it leads to generalization and categorization (some features of social identity theory).

• A study that investigated illusory correlation in the context of making judgements about individuals was conducted by **Hamilton and Rose (1980)**. They studied how illusory correlations maintain social stereotypes of particular groups or occupations. They conducted three experiments with undergraduate students and adult participants: 77 females and 73 males. In the first experiment, the volunteers were made to read adjectives and traits that described someone of a particular occupancy, with the inclusion of some non-stereotypical adjectives. The second experiment included adjectives that were either consistent or unrelated to the stereotypes of the occupational groups and in the third study the traits were inconsistent with the stereotypes of the groups. Participants were asked to estimate how often each of the traits described members of certain jobs or positions. The study showed a sign of systematic biases in the responses, as the participants associated the adjectives with the jobs in terms of their stereotypes instead of the actual causes. Noticeably, the participants ordered the new information by the stereotypical belief. Due to this, the researchers were certain that cognitive biases and stereotypes as such come from two rare events that occur simultaneously, and humans assuming that there must be an association between them (illusory correlation). This study clearly shows the process of how stereotypes are formed. The application of this study is that it can be used to identify stereotypical thinking and potential discriminative behaviour by showing the mechanism of this phenomenon. The study was made of volunteers, so the level of motivation was high; however, as these were students there could be an issue of sample bias. It would be difficult to generalize the findings of the study to other aspects of stereotypical thinking as only the occupation was taken under consideration in this case.

• **Stereotype threat as an effect of stereotypes (Forbes et al. (2018))**: 73 men and 87 women took part in the study. All of them knew the negative stereotype of women being inferior to men in maths. They were randomly allocated to stereotype threat or control condition; the first group was told that the test they were about to take would be significant in terms of their maths intelligence; the other group was told that it's about identification of their problem-solving abilities. Participants in the first condition were asked some questions in terms of demography, as well their gender; there was also one male experimenter who read the instructions. The control condition didn't include a gender question and there was a female experimenter reading instructions. All participants completed a maths task (multiplication/division) for over 30 minutes, during which feedback regarding their performance was provided; if participants were not able to complete the task, they received negative feedback, then a standard maths task was introduced for 5 minutes. The last part was a surprise memory test – its aim was to assess the extent to which participants encoded fonts associated with negative or positive feedback during the maths feedback task. Continuous EEG activity was recorded throughout the process. The results show that the women experiencing stereotype threat performed worse on the maths feedback task compared to other participants. The stereotype affected the activity of the amygdala (it was increased) in women (surprise reactions) caused by negative feedback during performance, was associated with increased connectivity between regions responsible for emotional memory coding during trial memory tests, in which they accurately recognized negative font-feedback pairings seen during the performance. This increased connectivity between regions of emotional memory and in turn allowed predicting better memory accuracy for pairs of negative feedback loops of fonts observed during the performance. This increased connectivity between regions of emotional memory in turn allowed predicting better memory accuracy for

pairs of negative feedback loops of fonts observed during the performance. These patterns were not visible in the correct feedback. This suggests that the stereotype that threatened women remembered negative feedback better because of stress-induced emotional memory processes. Men encoded negative feedback more accurately in the semantic memory.

Some arguments in discussion: it was an experiment with maths tasks, so it would be difficult to generalize the findings to other aspects of life. Bidirectional ambiguity could have an effect as it's not clear if the knowledge about stereotypes affects the performance or if the negative performance affects the women's self-esteem and induces stereotypes. On the ethical side, there could be psychological harm when it comes to self-assessment and the feedback given by researchers in the stereotype-based stress.

Set C: Paper 2 (SL and HL)

1. • Reliability in diagnosis means that two clinicians will diagnose the same patient with the same disorder when using the same diagnostic criteria.

• Validity of diagnosis refers to the extent to which a diagnosis given to a patient is 'correct' (i.e. when it allows appropriate identification of symptoms and therefore accurate treatment is incorporated).

• **Rosenhan (1973):** The aim of this study was to test the validity of diagnosis. Eight participants took part in the study, including Rosenhan. They were told to report hearing voices (thud, empty, hollow). All of the participants were admitted to different psychiatric hospitals in the USA. Each participant from then on acted normally, not presenting any other symptoms of mental disorders. All of them were admitted to the hospitals with diagnosed schizophrenia, with an exception of one participant diagnosed with manic depression. As patients, they took notes on their time being hospitalized; however, hospital staff interpreted it as a symptom of their illness. They were released after 7–52 days with a diagnosis of schizophrenia in remission (except one patient). After publishing the study, Rosenhan got messages from psychiatric hospitals claiming that it would never happen in their institution, so the follow-up study was conducted. In this variation, Rosenhan contacted hospitals and told them that he would send pseudo-patients. 41 real patients were suspected to fake their symptoms, 19 of which were suspected by a psychiatrist and a staff member; however, no pseudo-patients were sent. The study raised awareness of invalid diagnoses and had an impact on perceiving psychiatry. It prompted a revision of diagnostic procedures and discussion about consequences of diagnoses. The follow-up study could have caused issues as actual patients were 'recognized' as imposters, which could have negatively affected the treatment they had received. One can refer to sick-role bias, which means that hearing about symptoms can result in doctors diagnosing the patient with reference to classification systems and their previous experience.

• **There are some serious flaws of this study:** It was done in a different historical context and as a result has low temporal validity (the findings of this study could be questioned because of the fact that a different understanding of abnormal behaviour was manifested 50 years ago, when DSM-II was used as a classification system). The research method used was a naturalistic covert observation, which raises another important consideration in terms of replicability of the study. One can also analyse ethical considerations such as the fact that hospitals didn't sign informed consent and deception was implemented. Another methodological issue is the sample used in this study (only eight people participated, including Rosenhan, in what potentially could lead to confirmation bias). Hearing voices was the only symptom patients claimed to suffer from and DSM V (the recent version of the classification system) won't allow for a diagnosis of schizophrenia using only this symptom. Back in the 1970s, psychiatry and clinical psychology didn't have a good press and there was no strong awareness of ethical considerations (e.g. Milgram's and Zimbardo's experiments). Also, as this observation considered only one symptom of one mental illness, the possibility of generalization of results from this study is very limited.

• **Cooper (1972):** The aim of the study was to investigate reliability of diagnosis of depression and schizophrenia. The researchers asked American and British clinicians to diagnose patients age 20–59 by watching a number of videotaped clinical interviews. Depression was twice more often diagnosed by British psychiatrists while the same patients were twice more often diagnosed with schizophrenia by American psychiatrists. It showed that the same diagnosis method could result in different outcomes. It also points out that there could be cultural differences in the way that mental disease is perceived. Also the use of descriptive psychopathology appears to be subject to distortion by systematic bias.

- **Another important factor in validity and reliability of diagnosis are classification systems** (e.g. DSM-5 and ICD-11). These are created to help track specific patterns or symptoms in mental health. It means that clinicians should be able to use the same diagnostic manual and end up diagnosing the patient accurately. The diagnosis should be consistent and reliable. Clinicians diagnose patients by clinical examination – it refers to interviews, blood tests, brain imaging and also a conversation between the psychiatrist and the patient (self-assessment tools are used to assess the symptoms – this is a highly subjective and unreliable source of information as it is opened to memory distortion). One needs to remember about the confirmation bias (on the clinician side) and reactivity (the patient can behave differently because she/he is being examined by a specialist) which potentially could affect the outcome of diagnosis. A very important point is that if the diagnosis is reliable it doesn't have to be valid. In some cases, clinicians could overestimate the role of dispositional factors when diagnosing their patients; what is more, overpathologization/underpathologization could play a role as well. Comorbidity could also play a significant role in validity and reliability of diagnosis (some symptoms are similar between disorders; also patients could suffer from different disorders at the same time). Method triangulation could enhance the validity of diagnosis as applying different ways of examination could lead to more data and to a more complex conclusion.

2. • **Etiology** refers to causes/reasons of diseases. In terms of psychological disorders it focuses on different factors which can contribute to the start of the symptoms.
- Research made in the area of abnormal psychology is sensitive in many aspects, so ethical considerations need to be analysed.
- The possible **ethical issues** in the study of etiologies are: psychological undue stress/harm, anonymity and confidentiality, deception, debriefing with informed consent and right to withdrawal.
- **Klump et al. (2001):** The aim of the study was to examine genetic and environmental influences of Anorexia Nervosa in the group of adolescent twins. 672 female reared together twins took part in the study (16–18 years of age). Diagnoses were conducted by the use of clinical interviews and self-assessment questionnaires. Analyses showed that genetic and non-shared environments accounted for 74% and 26% variance in Anorexia Nervosa.
- **Ethical issues in this study could be** psychological harm, withdrawal, anonymity and informed consent. Undue stress or harm could have an effect on participants as the information which was obtained by researchers could be labelling for life resulting in a possible self-fulfilling prophecy in showing symptoms of AN. Withdrawal needs to be granted as participants need to know that they can resign from the study at any point. Also they can withdraw their data if they feel uncomfortable or threatened in any way. This leads to anonymity – none of the personal details should be revealed to the public unless agreed – genetic predisposition to AN could be a significant consideration when it comes to participants' personal life. Another important ethical consideration is to inform participants about the aim, procedure and results of the study – everything should be clear and informed consent should be signed at the beginning of the study with all relevant information included.
- **Caspi et al. (2003):** People who had short versions of the 5HTT allele showed more symptoms of depression in response to stressful life events. The effect was the strongest for those with more stressful environmental influences. Inheriting the gene was not enough to lead to depression, but if people experienced some stressful life situations it increased the likelihood of developing depression. The issue here is that the results of later studies are inconclusive in terms of the role of the 5HTT gene in depression.
- **Ethical issues in this study:** The most important ones are psychological harm and debriefing. The first one is significant as the information about the results of the study and that the person has a shorter version of 5HTT allele could lead to self-labelling and thinking about depression as something

that will happen either way and the person doesn't have any control over it. Participants must be informed that it's not about 5HTT allele alone, but it's the effect of both environmental and genetic factors that potentially could lead to depression. Also participants should be informed about other studies not being so conclusive on this matter.
- **Some general ethical considerations** in terms of etiology and the studies which investigate it could refer to the way of measuring the probability of suffering from depression, as well as measuring symptoms. It's not possible to say with 100% certainty that one will/won't suffer from major depressive disorder in the future regardless of the reasons which are investigated. Another concern is the way the symptoms are identified, as in most cases participants are not diagnosed but symptoms are identified so as a result participants don't get any help through the form of professional treatment.

3. • Culture is defined by **Matsumoto & Juang (2004)** as a dynamic system of rules, explicit and implicit, established by groups to ensure their survival, involving attitudes, values, beliefs, norms and behaviours.
- **Sue & Zane (1987):** One of the most important aspects of culture in treatment is how credible the treatment is. Asian culture has a specific attitude towards other members of society, especially when it comes to credibility in terms of treatment. Achieved credibility refers to a therapist's skills, so if a therapist is skilful it could lead to trust, confidence and hope from the client's point of view. For example, Asian cultures could perceive young female therapists as having expertise but low status because of their age and gender. A mature experienced therapist will be perceived as having high ascribed credibility but low achieved credibility.
- **Dadlani & Scherer (2009):** Self-awareness about one's values, beliefs and reflexivity is important when it comes to the therapy relationship between client and therapist, as therapists need to develop a critical mind-set that refers to skills, attitude, cognition and emotions. There is also an expectation from therapists to acquire the knowledge about diverse populations before the beginning of the therapy; some questions can be asked during the treatment to understand culturally specific behaviours. Culturally specific interventions should also be taken under consideration (e.g. the treatment is translated into the language of the group in question). Some interventions should also be culturally adapted to make sure that beliefs and values of cultural groups are incorporated (this potentially can lead to understanding, trust and bigger engagement in the therapy). However, the studies provided contradictory results in this matter (racial identity, level of acculturation, understanding between therapist and client).
- If the client's problems are conceptualized in an incompatible way with client belief systems, the therapist's credibility is reduced. If the therapist expects responses that are culturally incompatible or unacceptable, or if there is a significant discrepancy between the aims that the client and therapist want to achieve, then the credibility achieved by the therapist is reduced.
- **Nicholl & Thompson (2004):** The study focuses on psychological treatments of PTSD among adult refugees. This meta-analysis, however, based on a limited amount of research to date indicate that culturally specific adaptations of CBT seem significant in terms of previously mentioned factors, as well as the effectiveness of treatment. The therapist has to be properly trained and aware of all possible culture-bound considerations when implementing treatment.
- **Hinton et al. (2011):** The aim of the study was to examine the therapeutic effect of a culturally adapted version of CBT (CA-CBT) for PTSD in comparison to applied muscle relaxation (AMR) in the group of Latino patients (women) with treatment-resistant PTSD. Participants were randomly allocated to groups which received either CA-CBT or AMR. Symptoms were assessed before treatment, after treatment, and after 12 weeks of follow up. The treatments were operationalized in the form of group therapy during 14 weekly sessions. The assessment was based on the measurement of PTSD, anxiety and culturally relevant idioms of distress, as well as emotion regulation ability. There was a significant difference in the number of symptoms in CBT in comparison to the AMR condition. The results showed a significant reduction in PTSD symptoms in the CA-CBT group but only slight improvement in the AMR group. The results suggest that CA-CBT can be beneficial for previously treatment-resistant PTSD in Latino women.

4. • **Developing as a learner** can be explained as a systematic contact with the environment (experience) which results in changes to people's skills, thinking and behaviour.
   • Many classic studies were conducted in the previous century. The most widely used research method has been an experiment as it is the most strictly controlled research method, as a laboratory one also should allow to identify IV and DV, as well as a cause-and-effect relationship to be established. Another research method used in this area of psychology is a correlational study, which investigates naturally occurring events with the use of brain-imaging technologies to identify changes in brain development.
   • **Piagets' theory** of cognitive development identifies several stages of development, one of the assumptions being that children at some point of their life are egocentric, meaning that children are not able to see the situations from other peoples' point of view (children assume that other people experience the world exactly the same way as they do). Piaget wanted to investigate egocentrism in the pre-operational stage of development.
   • **Piaget & Inhelder (1956):** Children of different ages took part in the study (4–7 year olds). Children were presented with a model of three different mountains, then the doll was put in different places at the table. Participants were presented with ten pictures of mountains taken from different angles and asked to indicate which picture showed mountains from the doll's perspective. Results showed that 4-year-old children chose a photograph of what they saw, not taking under consideration the different point of view. 7- and 8-year-old children chose the picture which showed the mountains from the doll's perspective.
   • This study used a laboratory experiment as a research method. The justification of its use was that the cause-and-effect relationship could be identified, which wouldn't be possible when using correlational study or any type of observation. The age was a significant variable in this experiment, which makes the results of the study less causal and more correlational. Another factor in discussion is artificiality (meaning that the settings of the study were not natural and it is impossible to predict what would happen in real life – the behaviour of participants was unnatural) and ecological validity (whether or not researchers can generalize their findings from observed behaviour in the laboratory to the outside environment). Other studies (e.g. **Hughes (1975)**) show contradictory results and question the procedure and settings of the study.
   • **Chugani (2001):** The aim of the study was to investigate the effects of early deprivation on brain development. Researchers applied PET scans in ten children (six boys and four girls, with an average age of about 9 years old). Children were adopted from Romanian orphanages. Earlier studies showed signs of poor cognitive abilities. Chugani decided to use two control groups (17 healthy adults and 7 children with a mean age of 10 years old suffering from epilepsy). The results showed significant changes in the group of orphans – mild neurocognitive impairment, impulsivity as well as attentional and social problems were reported. In comparison to both control groups, there was a decrease in glucose metabolism in amygdala, hippocampus and prefrontal cortex. Researchers claim that these brain structures are very sensitive when it comes to environmental influences, such as continuous stress. In this case the brain parts with decreased glucose metabolism which may have been affected by early deprivation and could have resulted in behavioural, cognitive and emotional changes in the long term.
   • The research method used was a quasi-experiment (no IV was manipulated, participants were not assigned randomly to conditions) correlational study. Basing on brain imaging technology (PET) specific changes in the brain are visible; however, there is no way a cause-and-effect relationship can be established; PET is an invasive technique and also has low temporal resolution, so quick processes are not easily detected. The sample was small. Also the characteristics of the sample could lower the possibility of generalization of the results to different populations. Regardless of the results of the study, it is possible that there were other factors/variables which were responsible for the brain changes visible on the PET scan. However, this research method was the best as it helped to collect data and to measure the potential relationship between two naturally occurring variables. Also as the topic of the study was sensitive it would be unethical to conduct an experiment with regard to the given aim.

5. • Child development is affected by many internal and external factors, peers and play being among them. Peers help us to socialize, to resolve conflicts, control emotions, communicate – this is how we become the member of society. Along with peers comes the play: Vygotsky (in terms of imagination and capacity of combining things) and Piaget (assimilation and accommodation) were studying it many years back. We are able to master our motor skills, sense of sharing, trust, our opinions, beliefs are created through it. Our decision-making and problem-solving skills are mastered, we learn how to read, write and count. Play is learning.
   • **Russ et al. (2004)** used APS (affect in play scale) which measures imagination, affect themes and enjoyment on a scale of 1 to 5. The APS is based on a 5-minute play task (building blocks and puppets). The child is asked to play with puppets so they are making something together. In the study, school-aged children were engaged in five 30-minute play sessions. Single blind control was used as researchers didn't know about the control and experimental groups. Two experimental groups were used (imagination and affect) and one control group (puzzles and colouring). The study offered a variety of toys to the play groups whose play was attended by an adult trainer. Researchers asked the children to engage themselves in specific stories which focused on imagination (have a boy go to the moon) or affect (have a girl be happy at a birthday party). Children in the affect play group had a more positive and negative effect while playing; they also used their imagination more effectively and organized their stories better in comparison to the control group. The imagination group also exhibited positive changes when comparing to the control group. **Moore & Russ (2008)** conducted a follow-up study after 4 to 8 months and found that children from the imagination group improved their play skills even more over time.
   • **Carlson et al. (2013):** The aim of the study was to investigate the relationship between individual differences in executive functioning and pretense representational skills among preschool children. 104 preschool children (48 girls and 56 boys) and their parents took part in the study. Children were tested twice by a female researcher in 60-minute videotaped weekly sessions. Receptive vocabulary and short-term memory were tested and measures of executive functions and pretense tasks were used. Investigators were not aware of hypotheses of the study. Confounding variables were controlled (memory, verbal ability and appearance-reality distinction). Although correlational, results show that pretend play positively affects children's performance in executive function tasks. Executive functions were significantly related to pretence with all controls taken under consideration. It seems that pretend play can help children with different aspects of executive functioning (memory, thinking, attention, emotion regulation, decision-making, etc.). This could be an effective way to teach children to develop executive cognitive skills outside of school.
   • **The issue could be** a bidirectional ambiguity between executive functions and pretend play. Because of the nature of the study it is not possible to identify cause-and-effect relationships. Another issue in this study was the characteristic of the sample (demographic homogeneity). There also could be other factors which influence the relationship between executive functions and pretence, even with these controlled ones.
   • **Some general discussion of the role of play in development:** Much of the research done in this matter is correlational and old, so along with causality comes an issue with results and their reference to present times. There are many variables which need to be taken under consideration – they all contribute to the cognitive development, different RMs need to be used (experiments, correlational studies as well as longitudinal) to make sure that results of studies are not due to the research method used. Play is difficult to be measured, so standardized procedures should be implemented. Many studies are done in natural settings, which is positive in terms of participants behaviour. However, an uncontrolled environment could also lead to confounding variables which may influence the study. Studies should be done cross-culturally to determine the possible effect of cultural influences. Some of the studies done are cross-sectional and do not observe long-lasting changes in terms of the effect of play on cognitive/social development, which limits the conclusions to the short-term effects.

6. • **Theory of mind (ToM)** is the cognitive ability of recognizing mental states as my own and others. It also refers to the capability to understand that other people's mental states could be different from my own.

- Another important term in the context of ToM is metallization, which refers to deducing mental and emotional state using different sources of information (body language, verbal clues, the knowledge about the given person and our own past experience). Some evidence suggests that higher metalizing skills (e.g. generating a representation of another person's belief) that are based on integration of different types of knowledge (beliefs and emotions) are connected to the ability to empathize with others. A person needs to first observe then share and finally understand one's emotions to fully empathize. It may mean that people have a tendency to simulate others' mental and emotional state to make sense of their behaviour.

- **Cassels (2010):** Researchers investigated empathic concern and personal distress in East Asians and European Canadians. 190 female high school and university students took part in the study. To measure cognitive and affective empathy, the interpersonal reactivity index (Likert scale) was used. Analysis of self-assessment responses to questionnaires showed that the Western sample reported higher levels of empathic concern; however, their level of personal distress was lower in comparison to East Asian counterparts. The results of this study are in line with other studies done on young children (e.g. **Trommsdorff (1995)**; the study done on 212 5-year-old pre-school children); it can be suggested that emotional responses that are more prosocial could result from greater levels of these behaviours in Western cultures. This research shows some sociocultural factors in the development of metallization and empathy.

- **There are some limitations of this study:** The research method used was a questionnaire – self assessment (subjectivity, social-desirability effect). Gender bias could be an issue – only females took part in the study. The Asian sample could also be perceived as bicultural so it could have had an effect on the results of the study.

- **Hooker et al. (2008):** The aim of the study was to identify the neuronal mechanisms involved in another person's emotional responses and to study to what extent the activity of these neuronal mechanisms is associated with empathy. 20 young adults took part in the study. They completed IRI self-report questionnaires and then were asked to predict the emotion of characters. One of them had a false belief and one had a true belief (participants were put under fMRI scan throughout the task). Participants were asked to predict what emotion a character with false belief would experience if he/she had a more accurate understanding of the situation. According to fMRI scans, emotionally 'sensitive' brain regions showed more activity (medial prefrontal cortex, frontal gyrus and thalamus). The activity of said brain structure was significantly related to a higher perception of self-assessed empathy. Hooker and colleagues claim that when we predict an emotional reaction of another person, we tend to create an internal representation of this reaction. These representations help us to understand what other people feel which makes empathy more probable.

- **Evaluation:** Several emotions were projected on the pictures, not all of them were related to empathy. Self-reported questionnaires were administered, which can result in a biased response. Participants filled out questionnaires before they were scanned with fMRI, which potentially could have skewed the neural responses visible on the brain scans.

7. - **Dispositional factors** play a significant role as determinants of health. Genetic factor and personality will be discussed as such. Genetic predisposition seem to influence our behaviour in different areas of life (e.g. alcohol consumption). Some personality traits (personality is a sum of our beliefs, feelings, behaviours, thoughts – it makes us who we are) seem to contribute towards addictive behaviour.

- **LaBrie et al. (2014):** The aim of the study was to investigate if personal traits affect alcohol drinking behaviour. 470 students took part in the study (online questionnaires about daily drinking habits and negative consequences of drinking as well as a measure of impulsivity and sensation seeking was applied). Results showed that higher levels of impulsivity and sensation seeking are related to drinking. Strong beliefs about alcohol and sensation seeking correlated with greater alcohol use. Students with high negative urgency along with strong beliefs about the role of alcohol in their life correlated with negative consequences of alcohol consumption. The results of this study show clear correlation between dispositional factors (personality) and health problems.

- **The application of this study** could refer to some intervention strategies or alternative activities for students high in impulsivity

and sensation seeking. Some therapies could be implemented for those who find alcohol salient in the context of stress related behaviour.

- **Limitations:** The study is based on questionnaires. The study is correlational. Psychology students from private university were participating – so sample and response bias was possible. Longitudinal, cross-cultural studies should be used to investigate more diverse sample and possible changes in students' behaviour in the long run.

- **Tabakoff et al. (2009):** Twelve participants with opiate dependency history took part in the study (eleven men, one woman). They were opiate free at the time of the study (confirmed by urine testing). They listened to two short autobiographical stories: one of them described a neutral episode, the second one described the situation when the participants were craving for opiates. At the time of listening to both scripts they were put under the PET scan with the use of a radioactive tracer to track changes of cerebral blood flow. Eight participants showed signs of craving in the left medial prefrontal region, left orbitofrontal cortex and adjacent left anterior cingulate cortex. The length of abstinence showed a significant positive association with the size of the difference in cerebral blood flow between two conditions in the left anterior cingulate. Orbitofrontal cortex seems to play an important role in drug addiction as it is linked to a mesolimbic system and reward pathway.

- This study is correlational in nature: no causation is identified. The amount of people is limited. Gender bias appears. There are no control participants to compare the results. PET is an invasive, artificial and correlational brain imaging technique. There could have been an issue of bidirectional ambiguity in terms of brain changes and addiction.

- The use of dispositional factors in determining health behaviour is beneficial as it focuses on one aspect of the phenomenon and helps to isolate other variables; however, the use of an eclectic approach to health problems (e.g. addiction) would help to analyse the problem from different perspectives, as situational factors are also significant. Not all people with the above personality traits will become alcohol dependant, and studies using brain imaging need to be carefully analysed.

8. - Prevalence, sometimes referred to as prevalence rates, is the percentage of people in a population who have a specific disease or trait at a certain point or time.

- Incidence is the percentage of new cases in the population at any given time.

- **Goisis et al. (2015):** The aim of the study was to investigate the role of income inequalities on childhood obesity. Over 19,000 UK children took part in the study. Data was collected during home interviews (questions about socioeconomic status and health-related behaviours were asked) when cohort members were 5 and 11. The first variable indicated if the child had gone from being normal weight at the age of 5 to overweight/obese at the age of 11 or from overweight to obese. The second variable indicated if the child had gone from obese at the age of 5 to being overweight/normal weight at age 11, or change from being overweight to normal weight. Prevalence of obesity was considerably higher among the poorest children in comparison with children with the top income. Difference in income was statistically significant for obesity at age 5, for overweight and obesity among 11-year-old children. The size of income inequality in obesity among children and being overweight increased between 5 and 11 years of age. The poorer children were more likely to move upwards through weight categories than richer children. The results of the study show that risk factors which increase prevalence of obesity among young children should be targeted at the early years as the family environment has a more significant effect on children's development early in life.

- **Criticism:** Millennium Cohort Study data was used – the sample is representative. The results didn't allow for a cause-and-effect relationship between obesity and income inequalities. Mothers reported about their children's health behaviours (subjectivity and possible lack of awareness of 11-year-old healthy behaviours). The study was longitudinal. The study was done only in one culture – the UK.

- **Baskind et al. (2019):** The aim of the cross-sectional study was to investigate the relationship between parent-perceived stress and risk of child obesity. The study was done in USA Massachusetts with the use of surveys. 689 pairs of parents and children participated. Parents were asked questions about their subjective perceived stress (how much stress do you feel in your life? Five options of response were given). Researchers investigated associations between parents' stress and children's BMI and obesity-related behaviour. Among overweight children and with obesity, parent-perceived stress was associated with fast-food consumption and physical activity. The reason could be that stress relates to meals high in fat and sugar that in turn could be related to not eating healthy at home and in turn buying fast foods. Parent-perceived stress also correlated with the BMI of children from low-income groups.

- **Criticism:** Only one question was used to measure perceived stress, which can be perceived as a limitation because the question was not specific enough. However, the Washington Institute of Medicine recommended a measure of a single item instead of a long measuring tool. The possible issue could have been a sampling bias as a high perception of stress could have resulted in them not being willing to participate in the study or making it difficult to reach them. The study was based on surveys – subjective information from parents was gathered, which could have resulted in biased responses (social desirability effect). The study was done only in one culture – the USA. Objective measures of cortisol levels could have been applied as well. The study was cross sectional, which means that it didn't show long-term changes in children's behaviour.
- **To sum up the discussion:** Data was gathered through self-reported measures which are subjective and not fully reliable. Many external and internal factors (risk and protective factors) should be taken under consideration when discussing prevalence of health problems (addiction, obesity, stress). Most studies are correlational in nature. Cross sectional studies don't refer to long-term changes; on the other hand, longitudinal studies show ongoing changes. However, many other variables could account for these differences.

9. - Health promotion targets unhealthy behaviours by changing peoples' habits, thinking and attitudes. Health promoting interventions try to implement some changes to already existing behaviours or prevent unhealthy habits from happening.
- Different research methods (quantitative and qualitative) are used to investigate healthy and unhealthy behaviours in societies. The ones contrasted: experiment and focus groups. Studies used: experiment (**Campbell et al. (2008)**) and semi-structured interviews (**Herbec et al. (2014)**).
- **Campbell et al. (2008):** 10,730 12–13-year-old students from England and Wales took part in the study. 29 schools were randomly allocated to the control group and 30 schools were allocated to the intervention group. The intervention was based on ten weeks of training influential students to act as supportive peers during informal interaction to encourage peers not to smoke, solve problems and general support. Observation followed immediately after the intervention and after 1–2 years. All participants were asked to complete a questionnaire about young people's smoking behaviour; a saliva sample was taken from students to limit the level of subjectivity. Results showed a 22% reduction in the odds of being a regular smoker in an intervention school compared with a control school. The study showed that the ASSIST health promotion programme was effective in the reduction of regular smoking in adolescents for two years after its delivery.
- **Herbec et al. (2014):** The aim of the study was to investigate the expectations of pregnant women seeking online stop smoking programmes with reference to internet-based smoking cessation intervention. 13 UK pregnant women who completed the pilot version of ISCI 'Mums Quit' took part in this study (a four-week automated program which provides behavioural support from an expert advisor). Each participant took part in one 35-minute telephone interview. Interviews were quite flexible and asked open-ended questions about reasons of joining the trial, women's views of the programme, as well as their suggestions of how ISCI could be used to target pregnant smokers. Interviews were recorded and transcribed. Theme analysis helped to identify six main themes: participants preferred ISCI to be engaging, include comprehensive and motivating content and features supportive of the quit process, be targeted to pregnancy, feature tailoring of structure and advice, and offer personal contact.
- **General evaluation** of both studies could refer to: gender and age distribution, ethical considerations, cultural considerations, application of findings, and sample/sampling method characteristics.

Contrast of research methods:

Natural experiment, Campbell et al. (2008)	Semi-structured interview, Herbec et al. (2014)
Quantitative research method providing quantitative data.	Qualitative research method providing qualitative data.
Personal contact was implemented between peer supporters and student participants.	Telephone interview was used (no personal contact).
Objective results in the form of percentage, previous hypothesis could affect conclusions.	Thematic analysis was used (no theoretical assumption before; however, opened to subjectivity).
Measures of health promotion effectiveness are easy to be implemented. The most widely used research method in health promotion.	Opinions, attitudes and beliefs are provided as answers.
IV and DV were identified but were not manipulated. Other confounding variables should be taken under consideration as this was a natural experiment.	No causation identified.
Results are based only on numbers.	Deeper insight into people's decision making and thinking processes in the context of smoking behaviour.
Researcher bias could affect the results of the study (double blind control could help).	Some responses could be the result of social desirability bias (smoking behaviour).
Control condition was used.	No participants were allocated to a control website.
1-year follow up and 2-year follow up were used in this experiment.	No follow ups in this study.

10. - Interpersonal relationships are affected by many factors as these are ongoing processes created by two human beings. Self-disclosure, conflict resolution methods and attribution, and communication styles all contribute to maintaining or changing/ending relationships.
- **Lawrence et al. (2008):** The aim of the study was to investigate patterns of change in global satisfaction among newlyweds (participants mean age: men, 25-years-old and women: 23-years-old). 502 spouses took part in the study; they were recruited by newspaper advertisements or invited by researchers (requirements: first marriage, married less than 6 months, no children). A large proportion of participants were full-time students. Consent was provided. Before the study, participants were asked to fill out individual questionnaires. Then participants took part in problem-solving discussions and completed additional measures. Marital satisfaction, relationship problems, verbal aggression, negative attribution and self-esteem was assessed eight times over the four years of each study, once every six months. Acute stress was measured at the first six assessments. Researchers used different surveys and questionnaires to gather data. 58% of husbands and 69% of wives showed a high and stable satisfaction level throughout the first four years of marriage. Partners with the lowest marital satisfaction showed relatively high initial levels of relationship problems, verbal aggression and acute stress; they were also characterized by low self-esteem. Partners who claimed lower levels of satisfaction at the beginning of the marriage were at a bigger risk of negative marital outcomes. In the first four years, spouses characterized with the low satisfaction had marital dissolution rates three to four times higher in comparison to spouses from the moderate and high satisfaction groups. Identified variability so early in marriage (couples had been married for less than six months) suggests that the individual differences in satisfaction and other domains are likely to appear a long time before the start of the marriage.
- **Evaluation:** Sample issues (young age, good education, race), limited variability (strength and limitation), the study was done in a central Florida community (major state university). More diverse samples needed. Number of assessments and sample sizes could have affected groups responses. Individual subjective assessments

don't have to reflect population responses – generalization is limited as the sample is not fully representative. The study was longitudinal – long-term changes were observed. Trends were identified. The results were in line with earlier studies; however, older studies were using different measurement methods. The study was done in Western culture, whereas marital satisfaction could be perceived differently in Eastern collectivist cultures. Self-assessment methods were used to gather data. No cause-and-effect relationship was established. The results of this study help us understand why relationships change or end.

- **Lavner, Bradbury, Karney (2012):** The aim of this study was to investigate relationship skills and/or behaviours and their potential role in marital satisfaction. 101 newlywed couples (18–55 year olds) were recruited through marriage license records on the suburbs in the Midwest USA. Couples dated an average of 48 months prior to marriage. After three months of marriage couples were asked to complete a marital adjustment test (MAT) (self-report measure), then participants were asked to come to the laboratory and a relationship domains interview was administered to them. This was a 60-minute individual semi-structured interview covering interactional domains in the context of the quality of couple's functioning (intimacy, support, decision-making, sexual relationship, communication and conflict). After 9–12 months, 21–24 months and 30–33 months of marriage, couples completed MAT again. Only three out of the five factors (sex, decision-making and control, and communication/conflict management) predicted rates of change in husbands' marital satisfaction, and quality of the sexual relationship was a significantly stronger predictor compared to other factors. Communication and conflict management uniquely predicted changes in marital satisfaction. Conflict management was a significantly stronger predictor in comparison to other factors.
- **Evaluation:** The study was correlational. It was based on a theoretical background. Spouses were giving different (but related) information on their relationships – as questionnaires are subjective self-assessment tools. The application of the study could refer to potential prevention programmes in the context of marital dissatisfaction and distress. Only heterosexual married couples were studied – generalizability issues. Sample size was small. The study was longitudinal. Different factors were taken under consideration. The use of semi-structured interviews is a strength as this research method is quite flexible and allows interviewees to talk freely (similar to everyday conversation) – social desirability bias should be analysed. Some parts of the study were done in a laboratory (artificiality, ecological validity and reactivity should be analysed).
- **General discussion of research:** Both studies are prospective – it's possible to see changes as a relationship continues, unlike prospective studies which are not fully reliable (e.g. memory distortion). Both studies took different factors under consideration. Informed consent, right to withdraw, anonymity/confidentiality should be obtained as most topics are sensitive and personal. Bidirectional ambiguity is possible as most studies are correlational.
- **Altman & Taylor (1973)** theory, **Fincham & O'Leary (1983)** and **Gottman & Levenson (1986)** studies could be used in this response as well. However, they would be used in the context of changing or ending of relationships.

11. • Prejudice is a combination of affection and cognition. It is an emotional (mostly negative) attitude towards an individual or a group which derives from judgement based on characteristics of a given group/person.
- **Integrated threat theory** consists of realistic threats (political, financial, physical), symbolic threats (psychological differences between groups), negative stereotypes (out-group threats), and intergroup anxiety (subjective fear during interaction with out-group members). This theory is seen in **Tausch et al. (2009)**.
- **The stereotype content model:** Two dimensions in the context of in-group/out-group – feeling of warmth (trustworthiness, sociability, friendliness) and competence (being capable and assertive). This theory is seen in **Fiske et al. (2002)**.
- **Fiske et al. (2002):** The aim of the study was to investigate if competence and warmth differentiate our group stereotypes and, as a result, prejudice. Three studies using eight samples were performed; about 400 undergraduate psychology students and non-students took part in the study. They were asked to complete self-administered, open-ended questionnaires at home and to rate groups on scales 1 to 5 reflecting warmth, competence, perceived status and perceived competition. The

instruction was: 'Off the top of your head, what various types of people do you think today's society categorizes into groups (i.e. based on ethnicity, race, gender, occupation, ability, etc.)? In the space below, please list between eight and sixteen such groups.' General results showed that the status perceived by participants correlated with competence perceived; however, perceived competition predicted perceived lack of warmth. These help to understand stereotype contents and prejudiced affects.
- **Criticism:** Out-groups were chosen by researchers not by participants which is a strength in terms of standardization, but it could also mean that this choice affected the results (researcher bias). Students took part in the study – sample bias. Participants were asked to answer question from the perspective of the society; however, it is not possible to say if they did.
- **Tausch et al. (2009):** 87 Hindu and Muslim psychology/sociology students took part in this study. They were asked to complete the questionnaire about Muslim-Hindu relations in India. Measured predictor variables were: contact quantity, perceive relative status; mediator variables: realistic threats, symbolic threats, intergroup anxiety; criterion variables: social distance, in-group bias, intergroup anxiety and realistic, but not symbolic, threat emerged as predictors of prejudice and partial mediators between the predictor and criterion variables. These findings were qualified by majority (Hindu) versus minority (Muslim) group membership. Symbolic threat was a predictor of prejudice for Hindu participants; realistic threat was the most significant predictor for Muslim participants. In-group status was as a significant predictor for the low-status minority group only. The findings suggest that integrated threat theory could be a useful theoretical base for understanding prejudice predictors. Understanding the role of different threats in a given inter-group context and identification of potential threats could help to apply anti-prejudice social programmes.
- **Evaluation:** The study was cross-sectional – no cause effect relationship. Self-assessment measures were used. There were sample issues – there were a low number of participants who were psychology students.
- **General discussion:** Both theories and studies approach stereotypes and prejudice in a reductionist way as we can't be sure if these are the only possible dimensions in stereotypes; different factors and perspectives should be taken under consideration (social, cultural, biological, cognitive). These studies provide only correlational links. Stereotypes which eventually lead to prejudice and discrimination serve as a cognitive shortcut in making sense of the world, as we don't have to acquire a lot of information about the person or group of people to understand his/her behaviour.

12. • Biological perspective assumes that prosocial behaviour has chemical (neurotransmitter serotonin) and/or evolutionary roots (kin selection theory).
- **Serotonin** is an inhibitory neurotransmitter related to sleep and mood regulation; however, some researchers have investigated it in the context of prosocial behaviour.
- **Crockett et al. (2010):** The aim of the study was to test the role of neurotransmitters in moral judgment and behaviour: it used the so-called trolley problem. The experiment used repeated measures and was counter-balanced; 30 participants took part in the study. First condition: participants were given SSRI drug (citalopram) – it blocks reuptake of serotonin from synaptic gap and increases the amount of neurotransmitter. Second condition: participants received placebo instead of active substance. Third stage: participants had to deal with a series of moral dilemmas (saving five lives vs killing an innocent person). Aversive harmful situations were divided into personal (being personally involved by pushing the person off the bridge to stop the train and save five people) and impersonal (pressing the lever to change the path of the train (hitting one person instead of five). Researchers found the decisions made in personal conditions were affected by the drug (citalopram) – participants were less willing to push the person off the bridge to save more people. The moral judgement was not affected in an impersonal condition. The results showed that serotonin plays a role in prosocial behaviour as it affects our judgement, especially when it comes to personal harm. As a result, we are more prone to help as the amount of serotonin and its effect is enhanced by the SSRI drug. Results also could mean that trait empathy measures may predict whether patients are likely to respond to SSRI treatment and imply that such treatments are less likely to be effective in psychopaths and patients with vmPFC damage.

- Researchers claim citalopram caused nausea in the group of participants, so some signs from their body could have helped them to identify which condition they are in (despite double blind control), which could have resulted in demand characteristics. The study used chemicals to alter the functioning of a human being (it was invasive); however, all participants agreed to take part in the study. There could have been an issue with the amount of citalopram as the dose could have been higher than the natural amount and it was not administered artificially.
- **Hysek et al. (2014):** 32 students (16 men and 16 women) took part in the study (repeated measures, double blind control). All 32 subjects were treated with MDMA and placebo (study was approved by the ethics committee, participants signed informed consent). Subjective effects related to prosociality (including feeling happy, open and close to others) were measured along with subjective mood effects. MET was used to measure empathy and the SVO test was used to assess social behaviour. The results showed that MDMA increased emotional empathy and prosocial behaviour. This effect was observed mainly in men. Male subjects showed more empathic concern and lower competition and exhibited more prosocial orientation after MDMA treatment, equal to that observed in women with placebo. Moreover, MDMA increased the preference for fairness and prosociality in men in a behavioural task.
- **Evaluation:** MDMA (ecstasy) was used – an addictive drug which could have an effect on participants (addiction, side effects). At some point participants could have realized which condition they were in as they experienced subjective effects of a drug. The study used chemicals to alter the functioning of human beings (it was invasive); however, all participants agreed to take part in the study.
- Kin selection theory predicts that altruistic acts are more likely to be directed towards relatives because of genetic similarity (**Madsen et al. (2007)**). The assumption of the theory is that we will help even at some cost, but if the reproductive potential is sustained it will be justified.
- **Madsen et al. (2007):** The study used repeated measures design; three experiments in total used the same scenario: participants were asked to do a painful physical exercise (sitting like a chair with their back against a wall, with the calves and thighs at right angles to each other) for as long as possible. The length of time participants maintained the position was calculated into a material benefit for a person, who was a relative to the participant. Only biological kin were included. Results showed a relationship between the effort put in the task and the relatedness of the person (participants stood in the painful position longer if they knew that the benefit would go to the closely related person). The results also showed that women may rely less on kinship cues than men do.
- There are no genes identified in the theory or study used; in most studies twins are used and asked to self-report their own reactions. This approach doesn't take the psychological aspect under consideration – why people spontaneously help strangers, what motivates them to do so? Low validity of KST. The study above was done to confirm the hypothesis – non-relative participants were not included.
- There are other significant factors which influence prosocial behaviour – reciprocity, moral and/or ethical obligations; however, isolating only one variable could be beneficial to test one theory.
- There is significant evidence that both neurotransmitters and evolutionary roots affect prosocial behaviour. However, one needs to remember that everything that is biological is psychological, so different areas should be investigated to get the full picture. Evolutionary explanations are not well investigated, and most theories are limited in predictive validity, not well empirically tested. Some evolutionary psychologists claim that people related to us are often close to us, which is why we help them, which is not an accurate assumption in present times. Analysing serotonin – both studies were artificial with the administration of a chemical substance – there could have been a demand characteristics so results could have been biased; also serotonin and SSRIs role/effectiveness is not conclusive according to results of various studies. One also needs to remember that besides biological altruism there is also a psychological one (based on our experience and cognitive processes).

Set C: Paper 3 (HL)

1a.
- The research method used was a semi-structured interview.
- This type of interview has a schedule. However, there is a possibility to add some new questions during the interview or change the order of the questions – there is room for flexibility (also when it comes the schedule itself).
- The most widely used questions are open-ended ones as they enable participants to elaborate on answers and respond more freely. Interviewees have a chance to provide an insight into their own experiences as this type of interview is more conversational in nature.

1b.
- The sampling method used in this study was purposive sampling.
- The researchers were looking for families with children who lived in a war zone (Gaza Strip) – specific characteristics of participants were crucial as researchers were investigating PTSD symptoms related to war-related trauma. This sampling method is a justified choice as it will help researchers to address a concern about the certain group of people. However, generalization is very limited (because of specific traits of the sample). Snowball sampling was applied as well as participants helped to find eligible friends and neighbours.

1c.
- One additional research method which could be used in this study is overt non-participant observation.
- The observation could be effective in children's natural environment (e.g. their home). The aim of these observations would be to identify potential symptoms of war-related PTSD. Accompanied by interviews, this research method could provide a different type of data, not only subjective self-relational, but also some observable behaviours which could serve as a method triangulation.

2.
- As the topic of the study is very sensitive and personal (trauma), researchers should take care of participants' anonymity. The reason for this is because of complicated political situations these families could potentially become labelled or ostracized as they reported some negative consequences of these attacks. None of the personal data should be revealed to the public (not only their names). Their identity should be protected. Reporting the results also means that all participants should agree for their data/responses to be used and published; if not, every family should have an opportunity to withdraw their data at any stage of the study (this information should be provided during debriefing). No pressure should be put on participants to keep their data in the study.
- To apply the results to another community, they would need to have characteristics similar to the sample being studied. Investigators shouldn't assume that the results can be generalized to different populations. It is crucial for the participants to stay anonymous; if any specific stories about children and families are published, none of the personal details should be revealed so that the children aren't identified. All participants should consent to use the results of the study, which include their data, to potentially help other families in similar situations (war-zone trauma), as the well-being of children is very important.

3.
- Credibility is the validity of the study. The first way to make sure that credibility is high is to ask participants to read and analyse their statements and check if these are correct along with their intentions and if necessary add some clarifications – in this study it would mean to ask families to read their responses as well as researchers' interpretations about PTSD.
- Researchers performed small observations while being at home, as well as questionnaires given to the mothers – so method triangulation was used. It increases credibility as different research methods provide different types of data. It is possible to check the consistency of the results and make sure that responses provided by participants during interviews were not biased because of possible demand characteristics.
- The sample which represents the whole population also increases credibility. In this study the sample (children and their mothers) was taken from a specific area of war. This means that they are not representative of the average child.
- Researcher triangulation could also increase credibility – its aim is to ensure that the data/results interpreted are accurate and not biased by possible personal opinions of the researcher (e.g. confirmation bias). Reflexivity also should be helpful in establishing credibility.

Printed in the USA
CPSIA information can be obtained
at www.ICGtesting.com
LVHW021817300723
753623LV00010B/225